Praise fo

BECOME THE INSPIRATION

"Real meaning in life never comes from games won, attention received, or the size of your paycheck. True contentment and joy are always the result of making a difference in someone's life. No better place to accomplish this and teach life lessons than in the athletic arena. It is the perfect microcosm of life. A coach can be the one who motivates young people to reach heights they never dreamed of, if he understands the responsibility that comes with his position and he checks his ego at the door. I have known Kurt Kreiter for 15 years. He gets it. He lives it. *Become The Inspiration* will motivate and help any coach build a program that inspires athletes to become the person that God intended them to be."

—*Mike Swider*
Head Football Coach at Wheaton College, Wheaton, Illinois
7X Division III National Qualifiers

"As I have climbed my way from small-town Iowa high school, walk-on to All Big-Ten, and now the NFL, I have sat and listened to many speeches from the best of the best. I have found one thing ‚in common in all of those speeches and lessons, and it's that I had already heard or experienced them. My father has given me all the tools I've needed to be a productive athlete and leader in life. His philosophy taught me these things in a way that made doing things the right way, the only way."

—*Casey Kreiter*
Son of Kurt Kreiter, NFL Player for the Denver Broncos

"Kurt Kreiter is a true competitor in life and sport who has developed his skills with Integrity, Honor, Commitment, Faith and Courage. I have watched him grow as a coach from both afar and close up. Kurt developed teams that were competitive into champions. I believe his greatest traits in building those champions the right way was through hard work, dedication and perseverance, not by skipping corners and having a win-at-all-costs attitude. Kurt went through lean years at the start to build the cornerstone of future champions, knowing that done the right way he would eventually succeed as a coach, mentor, and friend to his athletes. He instilled in his own coaching staffs, one of which I was very fortunate to be a part of, those same beliefs and character traits to carry on a winning tradition on and off the competitive arena. It is my belief that the true measure of a coach is one who truly cares about his athletes and not his own accolades. It is for that very reason I hold Kurt Kreiter in the highest regard as a coach, person, and friend."

—Kirk Azinger
Coach
Big Ten Wrestling Champion
University of Illinois, Champaign, Illinois

"Truly Coach Kreiter has coaching DNA in his blood. Coach Kreiter is a man of integrity and professionalism. He develops respect and pride in his coaches, community, and most importantly in his student athletes. Winning is always a goal, but only through competition with honor and integrity. He believes in the sound values we can gain through sports and activities. When the competition is over, friendship is more important than the rivalry.

—Tom Danner
Coach at Western Dubuque High School, Epworth, Iowa
2016 National Wrestling Hall of Fame

BECOME
THE INSPIRATION

LEADERSHIP PRINCIPLES AND FUNDAMENTALS FOR THE BEGINNING COACH

KURT L. KREITER

Foreword by Dr. Bryan Thomsen with Dr. Rick McGuire of the Missouri Institute of POSITIVE COACHING

Logo Artwork by Haley Kreiter, Champion, *2010 Iowa U.S. Fish & Wildlife Service Federal Junior Duck Stamp Art Competition*
Cover photo of Kurt Kreiter and Seth Klinefelter courtesy of *The Observer*, DeWitt, Iowa. Used with permission.
Interior photos courtesy of *The Observer*, DeWitt, Iowa. Used with permission.

Edited by Christine Gilroy.

To order multiple copies of this book for professional workshops, educational seminars, or staff copies, contact the author at the following email account:
1coachkreiter@gmail.com

For permission requests, contact the author:
Lone Oak Books
Kurt L. Kreiter
DeWitt, Iowa
coachkreiter@gmail.com

ISBN-13: 978-1543059212
ISBN-10: 154305921X

LONE OAK
BOOKS

TABLE OF CONTENTS

Foreword by Dr. Bryan Thomsen with Dr. Rick McGuire   vi
Preface   ix
Introduction   x

CHAPTER 1   So You Want to Coach   1
                   Developing Philosophy

CHAPTER 2   Keep Chipping Away   21
                   Program Development

CHAPTER 3   Building Leaders   34
                   Developing the Athlete

CHAPTER 4   Reach for the Stars   48
                   The Importance of Goals

CHAPTER 5   Feel Like a Champion   61
                   Developing Winners

                   Photo Section   84

CHAPTER 6   Building a Community   90
                   Establishing Your Program

CHAPTER 7   Making an Impact   109
                   Do the Work

CHAPTER 8   Inside Your Program   127
                   Little Things Can Make a Big Difference

CHAPTER 9   Beyond the Scoreboard   149
                   What It Is All About

                   Acknowledgments   162
                   About the Author   164
                   Information to Order Copies   166

FOREWORD

I grew up in a small rural community in eastern Iowa, where Main Street, local businesses, churches, farms, and sports defined the focus of our lives. My brother and I were always competing in sports in one way or another. Our backyard was transformed daily into a training ground for serious competition. Basketball, football, home run derby, and a variety of events were on the schedule each and every day. Oftentimes this serious competition ended up with some hand-to-hand combat training. We developed a love for sports and a desire to win. This, coupled with a strong work ethic learned from our parents, began to shape our athletic experience.

For my brother, basketball was his passion, but for me, football and wrestling meant nearly everything. I had lots of different coaches — different sports, different people, different philosophies, and different approaches. All of these had an influence on me, but there was one coach in particular, Coach Kurt Kreiter, who had a huge impact on me and upon my life. Coach Kreiter coached me in both football and wrestling, and he taught me a lot about sports and how to be a successful performer on the field and the mat. I loved playing for Coach Kreiter, and I would try to do anything and everything that he instructed or asked us to do. But for all that he taught me about becoming and being a better player, he taught me and showed me way more about being a great husband, father, and man.

My experiences in high school sports generally, and with Coach Kreiter specifically, led to opportunities that were beyond anything that I had dared to believe. After earning Junior College All American in football, I accepted a full scholarship to play for the University of South Carolina Gamecocks in the prestigious Southeastern Conference. This expanded my vision beyond sports. While not a strong, or even particularly interested, student in high school, I did earn my bachelor of science degree in criminal justice. When a career in the NFL was not a viable option, I turned my attention to applying the lessons I first learned under Coach Kreiter —preparation, personal investment, patience, persistence— to exploring and setting future career goals and gaining more education. Now with two master's degrees, one in education and one in parks and recreation administration, and a doctoral degree in educational administration, and with stints as a rancher, a teacher, and a principal, I am now passionate about my role as a superintendent of schools and leading a staff of nearly 200 professionals, all dedicated to teaching, caring, sharing, preparing, modeling, and winning in the lives of our kids.

I now understand what Coach Kreiter understood. It's not about football ... it's all about the football player! It's about making a difference in the life of every kid that you coach, whether you meet them on the athletic field, or in the classroom, or in the hallway.

In the past few years I have become a close friend and colleague of Dr. Rick McGuire, the retired head track and field coach and sport psychology professor at the University of Missouri. Dr. McGuire is also the founder and director of the Missouri Institute for Positive Coaching, with the stated mission of "Winning Kids With Sport!" Coach McGuire has provided our entire school staff with his "The Power of Positive Coaching Workshop." His message is powerful, and the principles of positive coaching that he teaches and espouses have literally been transformational for our teachers, coaches, administrative and support staff, and ultimately for the students in our schools.

I have personally become such a strong believer in the power of positive coaching that I have joined Dr. McGuire's Positive Coaching Team and travel with him throughout the country, delivering workshops, clinics, and keynote addresses encouraging coaches in sport at all levels to be positive coaches, to strive for excellence, to be demanding not demeaning, and to play to win. Yes, winning does matter, but it's not all that matters! But it absolutely does matter that we win in the life of every player, every person, every young girl or boy for whom we have the opportunity and the honor to serve as their coach.

I was that young boy! Coach Kreiter was my coach. He taught me a lot about football and wrestling, but he taught me more about being a husband, father, leader, and man. He showed me that the really great coaches are positive coaches. Coach Kreiter provided me with the inspiration. The building blocks of positive coaching are teaching, guiding, encouraging, building, believing, caring, sharing, giving, forgiving, expecting, respecting, modeling, serving, and inspiring. Coach Kreiter has created his road map and a challenge to all of us to be the inspiration.

Coach McGuire and I have read this fantastic book. We both love and endorse Coach Kreiter's message and his approach as a coach, a positive coach. This book should be a part of every new coach's philosophical foundation for truly helping kids be successful in sport and in life.

—Dr. Bryan Thomsen
Superintendent, North Callaway R-1 Schools
Kingdom City, Missouri
with
Dr. Rick McGuire
Founder & Director of the Missouri Institute of POSITIVE COACHING
University of Missouri
Columbia, Missouri

PREFACE

Much of my life, both personal and professional, has involved sports. As a youth, I could not wait to put on catching gear and get behind the plate. I long for the feeling of formfitting a running back during a football game or the anticipation of the collision when engaging the opponent from the front row of a rugby scrum. I can still sense the anxiety I felt prior to a wrestling match when it was I and I alone who was going to determine the outcome of that contest.

Many of those same feelings, anxieties, and emotions were still present as I coached. That may be why so many of us get involved in coaching after our competitive days. It is hard to find another way to replace that sports-induced vitality that makes us feel complete.

But maybe it is more than that. Maybe it is a way to tap into something more primitive that helps us feel alive and engages our senses. As we know, when that sense of involvement is missing in our lives, it can leave a big void. Beyond anything associated with talent or success, I am disappointed for all those individuals who did not get to enjoy that same experience because of the negative impact a coach might have had during those formative years.

Coaches in my life have been both inspirational and motivational. Because of the positive influence that coaches had on me over all of those years, I have enjoyed a lifetime of sports and made a lot of great memories in the process.

—Kurt Kreiter

INTRODUCTION

When building our programs, coaches often use knowledge that we acquire from other sources. This includes both useful and useless information, things we like and things we don't particularly care for, and the good and bad we experience on our journey. Personal experience, clinics, and books are some of the ways we gain the knowledge we need to build our foundation. From time to time, a coach may create something truly innovative and effective, but most of our philosophy, schemes, fundamentals, and drills are molded over the years by outside sources and our role models.

I wrote this book to share some thoughts, experiences, and insights into coaching that could be helpful to new coaches because we have so many common experiences in this profession. I hope you are able to take from this book something that is beneficial to your coaching career. I am not trying to reinvent the wheel, as they say. I am a fairly typical coach. I don't claim to know something that other coaches do not already know, nor have I developed a concept revolutionary to our field. I have experienced both success and failure as an athlete and as a coach. I don't always equate successful individuals, teams, and programs with championships won.

At the end of each chapter, I have included a writing labeled Game Day, a weekly message I used to publish each Friday of our football games. Game Day publicized a topic of choice that I wanted to share with those in and around our program. Now, as activities director, I prepare this wrap-up for the end of each sports season.

To me, nothing is more special than someone calling you "Coach." It is an honorable profession in which you can inspire greatness in others. Do it justice.

BECOME THE INSPIRATION

Chapter 1

SO YOU WANT TO COACH
Developing Your Philosophy

"The best leaders not only inspire us, they develop and empower us to lead with passion from whatever position we currently hold in life."

—Ty Howard

Little League baseball was my introduction to organized athletics. As with many other athletes, my first coach was my father, Jack Kreiter, who, along with Coach Tony Baker, started building a foundation for me in sports. To this day, these two volunteer coaches remain two of my greatest role models in coaching. That foundation set the stage for athletics to be an important part of my life for more than 40 years.

Sports have been an important part of my life as a competitor, coach, and now administrator. They have influenced almost every other part of my life. Coaching also has become something of a family business. My brother, Eugene, is a former high school head coach and my son, Casey, plans to coach again in the future. Growing up on a family farm in eastern Iowa, I thought I would become a generational farmer. But as it turned out, my parents insisted that my brother, sister, and I all attend college.

As with so many other endeavors in my life, I looked for a role model in education. When I was a high school sophomore, my high school biology teacher, Mr. Rick Moeller, made a positive impression on me. He was a tremendous teacher and coach. So at that time I decided I would follow in his footsteps and become a teacher and coach, too. The rest is history.

In college, I was highly influenced by one of my great mentors and role models, high school and college football Hall of Fame Coach Bob Reade, who got his start in coaching just down the road at a rival high school in Maquoketa, Iowa. He subsequently built a name for himself as a head football coach at the high school level in Geneseo, Ill., where he once had a 52-game winning streak while compiling a career record of 146-21-4, which included four state titles. I got a chance to play for Coach Reade while he was the head coach at Augustana College in Rock Island, Illinois. There, he amassed a career record of 146-23-1, including four straight national championships from 1983-1986 and 12 conference titles in the College Conference of Illinois and Wisconsin. As a transfer student from the University of Iowa, I had the privilege of playing for Coach Reade during the last three national championship seasons during a 60-game unbeaten streak. I graduated with seniors who did not lose a game during their college careers and won an unprecedented four national titles.

What all the records do not show is what kind of human being, man of character, and role model Coach Reade was. His record as a coach is nothing short of incredible at both the high school and college level, but his influence as a mentor far surpassed those records.

My time at Augustana College was both a blessing and a curse for me. The blessing was the influence that Coach Reade, such an important historic figure in sports, had on me. I was fortunate to have been part of something special, a type of success most athletes only ever dream of. It was an amazing experience and an achievement rarely found in any endeavor. It was also one that I experienced with an exceptional group of teammates. All the success was great, but the relationships and experiences with teammates and coaches transcended the titles won.

The curse occurred when I left Augustana and became a coach on my own. I was certain that creating a program with that kind of success would be as simple as Coach Reade had made it seem. As we all know, though, there is nothing simple about coaching or building a program with his kind of success. This realization has motivated me since that time.

Following my graduation from Augustana I entered the real world and took a job as a high school teacher and coach in a school not far from the family farm in rural Davenport, Iowa. I have spent the last 30 years at that school, Central DeWitt Schools in DeWitt, Iowa, serving as a classroom science teacher for 25 of those years and coaching in two of our high school athletic programs, football and wrestling. I have served as a coach at all levels in the program, including head coach. For the last five years I have taken on the ultimate leadership role in our activities program as activities director.

I would not have wanted to take on this role without the previous 25 years of hands-on experiences as a coach. During those years, I learned a great deal. As with other coaches, lessons I learned on the job were more useful in my education than my more theoretical formal education. I have found that now as an athletic director, I enjoy using those experiences in mentoring other coaches and sponsors, although nothing can replace coaching young people in the pursuit of their goals and dreams.

I now provide guidance and advice to our coaches about many of the situations I faced firsthand over my years of coaching, which has proved to be most rewarding. Many of these coaching situations are not unique to our school or to me alone, but are universal to all coaches.

To that point, I consider one of my greatest professional accomplishments taking a wrestling program that needed some work and turning it into a competitive program. During my first three years as head wrestling coach, our teams recorded a 4-42 dual meet record. My career record suffered 50 losses before getting 10 wins, and 100 losses before 50 wins. Had I been a little smarter, I might have turned things around sooner and not had to agonize over all the disappointments I was certain I was the first to experience. Had I been more realistic and less naïve, I would have saved myself some heartache and just quit.

But giving up was not in my nature. With great coaches, athletes, and a supportive community, I continued to build a solid foundation through all the adversity and over time turned the program into a winner. With the help of many, many others, I developed a program that our school and community could be proud of and a program young people wanted to be a part of. Wins, of course, were a natural result of that process, but what happened to the program during the 20 years I was head coach is something beyond a record, in which I take great pride

I have found that building a quality program may or may not require Coach Reade's level of success. You will work hard to build a championship team, but win or lose, it is important to construct a solid program first, one that will last and is built on a solid foundation. We have all watched teams experience great success, only to find out later that corners were cut and those in leadership positions were not running a clean program. There is nothing long-lasting when you win that way. A foundation built on deceit and unethical practice will never truly succeed. The winning will become hollow and all the time and effort wasted. What will be gained long-term if you win the wrong way and in the process fall far short in more important areas of your life like ethics and integrity?

We also have known coaches who have worked diligently to do things the right way, only to experience limited success in their programs. With today's increasing focus on winning, those programs may be short-lived as well. But even in defeat, you can take pride in knowing that you did not compromise your high ideals in the pursuit of victory. There is no shame in losing.

Ideally, you will continue to work hard and do the right things. You may face adversity over and over, but in time you will experience success because of the foundation you have worked to build. You will develop values in your program that will inspire long-lasting greatness in your individuals and teams. You will foster qualities such as commitment, responsibility, and respect as you focus on developing young people of high character. You may even be part of building or continuing long-standing traditions during your career. Coach Reade was able to accomplish great success and do it the right way. He also developed great traditions at both the high school and collegiate levels.

Here is what he once said about tradition:

"If you have a good program in high school, even when you don't have great material you should stay above .500. Then when you get the material you can go to the top. It's difficult to go from last to first no matter what kind of material you have. The key is to be consistently strong. The definition of a great program is not to win every game every year.

The definition of a great program is this: Anytime an opponent steps on your field, they know they will have to play their best or they will lose. When you get a program established, teams can't overlook you. They know it and your players know it. Even if you play below your ability, you still might win. That is TRADITION.

—Coach Bob Reade

WHY COACH

From the onset, you are likely to know that coaching is going to require a tremendous amount of physical and mental energy. It is also going to require a great deal of your time. Although the best in our business make it appear to be easy, it is not. Our experiences as athletes will give us only a clue as to what it is all about. As you decide to move up the ranks and take on higher positions within your programs, you will find that the time and energy required will continue to increase.

The mental strain can sometimes be the most dramatic of the changes. Things you may not have even considered putting much thought into as an assistant could require a great deal of your attention when you become a head coach. You will have to learn to deal with it or it will consume you. Before you commit to building a program and moving up the ladder, make sure you are honest with yourself and are committed for the long haul. Make sure you are prepared for it emotionally. If not, you may be setting yourself up for failure before even getting started.

Maybe you will run into significant roadblocks along the way. How do you plan to deal with overcoming those obstacles? You could potentially run into low numbers or talent issues. What plan will you implement to turn the ship around? Your program could be scrutinized if you don't meet expectations. How will you respond to that criticism? Maybe you lose a good assistant coach or someone on your staff becomes a detriment to your program. How do you address those issues? There are hundreds and thousands of "what ifs." You will likely have solutions to many of the problems that come your way much of the time, but you won't have all the answers all the time.

Because coaching is such a huge commitment, make sure you are coaching for the right reasons. When you do, you may find out that it will be one of the most rewarding experiences of your life. In any line of work, if you love what you are doing it will not seem like work. It becomes a labor of love. I knew from the time I decided I would enter the field of education that I wanted to become a coach. My initial interest was in being a coach, but I found out over time that I had a real passion for being a classroom teacher as well and took the same amount of pride in being an educator as I took in being a coach.

I started coaching before we had our own children, so I did not get involved only to have an influence on them. I just wanted to stay involved in something I loved that had made such an impact on me. When I began building a program as a head coach, I was more focused on building one that all athletes, including my own children, would be proud to be a part of, not just a program that my own children would benefit from. You will serve your athletes and their families better when you follow the Golden Rule: Do for others' children what you would do for your own.

You will be working with a family's most prized possessions, their children. You must first recognize that you have an enormous responsibility when working with young people, but you also have a responsibility to their parents. You should also recognize that you are going to have a great influence on them. The choice is totally yours whether that influence will be positive, inspiring, and potentially life changing — or negative, demoralizing, and potentially life changing. Choose right! Emulate the great mentors you had in your own life.

This does not necessarily mean to treat your athletes exactly as you would treat your own children, because maybe you are a little over the top with them. It also does not mean you mirror the behavior that was used by your own coaches, as possibly they used a less-than-thoughtful approach with you. What it boils down to is the difference between right and wrong. Treat your athletes the right way. The right way does include consequences, accountability, and high standards. But it also involves compassion, understanding, and mutual respect. The impact we make can be of even greater significance if students come into our programs initially lacking in these critical developmental areas.

There was a time in my career as an aspiring head wrestling coach when I decided I had had enough. I turned in my resignation during the season without discussing it with anyone. My brother, Eugene, who was coaching with me at the time, was shocked when our athletic director asked him what was going on. My wife, Jenny, was even more surprised. We finally had started to get things headed in the right direction, and our numbers had been getting better. By all outward appearances we were making good strides in the program. We anticipated filling a lineup for the first time in a few years. Then, out of the blue, one of our starters quit.

For some reason, that one young athlete making a decision to quit weighed heavily on my mind. As a driven coach, I had failed to develop a sense of perspective. From the time I got up in the morning until I went to bed there was some aspect of our program that was rattling around in my brain. This situation triggered something in me that has not happened often in my life — I gave up. Then a great mentor, athletic director, and successful coach, Pat Meade, sat me down and talked some sense into me, and I finished the season with a more positive attitude. He made clear to me what is not always apparent: Success can come in a variety of forms.

I realized my reaction had been a snap decision and I could not leave the program under those circumstances, letting the poor choice of an adolescent have such a negative influence on my life. That event did help me take one of the more important steps in my coaching career. It made me reevaluate why I had gotten into coaching in the first place and why I wanted to continue to be a coach. Understanding for the first time why I coached took some mental pressure off me and helped me refocus my negative energy into the pursuit of program goals and development of young people

There have been other situations, most often associated with adversity, that I have used to reevaluate the various aspects of my coaching career and the reasons why I coach. In each case, these challenges have made me a more effective coach and leader. Here are some things to think about when considering your involvement as a coach and whether you want the responsibility:

- You love the sport, you have been affected by it, and you want to give back.
- You can use your role as a positive influence on young people. A sport is a great extension of the classroom.
- You have the opportunity to nurture in athletes important personal qualities and characteristics that will serve them well for a lifetime.
- You are gratified watching young people mature and develop.

Of course, there are reasons that might deter you from coaching. You should consider these as well. Here is a short list:

- Are you a problem solver? You will need to troubleshoot various problems you encounter when working with young adults. Troubleshooting may include an occasional adult problem.
- Do you really know what the job entails? Coaches do much more than just coach today. Your job will involve

various other roles as a recruiter, videographer, stat keeper, information director, equipment manager, trainer, technology expert, and other duties.

- Do you have self-confidence? Many people will have an opinion about what you are doing and will not hesitate to let you know their thoughts. Ironically, in 25 years in the classroom, no one ever questioned a lecture or a lab I presented.
- Are you ready for the time commitment? You will need to invest a great deal of time that will often extend beyond your contracted time. It may also include year-round activities.

CORE VALUES & PHILOSOPHY

For the athletes who remain committed to your program and do what is asked, you should be responsible for providing a consistent experience. For the parents who entrust their son's or daughter's care to your coaching staff, there should not be a variation in the way they are treated depending on wins or losses. The guiding principles that direct your program should remain the same regardless of a record. That consistency is critical for long-term success and begins with your philosophy.

The development of a comprehensive philosophy can help you in the decision-making process and ultimately in building your program. Your philosophy will be the cornerstone in the foundation of your program. Developing a philosophy that you believe in will help guide you in almost every aspect of your program. Your philosophy is based on the ideals that you would never sacrifice and incorporates your core values. It is the principles you truly believe in. These will help guide you whether building success or overcoming adversity. You don't want your philosophy to end up being just a bunch of empty words or statements on a sheet of paper, so put some substance behind it and eventually turn your words into action.

I once broke open a fortune cookie only to find the little statement that read something like this: "Let a few strong beliefs and some basic instincts help guide you in life." I am a science-minded person so I don't believe that pseudoscientific principles are guiding my life in any way, but this statement made a lot of sense to me when I read it. I tucked it away into my wallet, and read it from time to time when I would run across it. It became one of those mental triggers that helped me remember that the foundation I was trying to build should be based on the philosophy or core values most important to me.

We don't have a professional football team in Iowa, so fans around the state rally around our college football programs during the fall. I grew up a Hawkeye fan and got to experience one of the great thrills as a father and coach when my son played football at the University of Iowa for Head Coach Kirk Ferentz, not only a successful coach but also one of the most respected college football coaches in the country. A man of high character, Coach Ferentz is well known for running a solid program and developing talent.

Like all other coaches, Coach Ferentz has experienced the highs and lows of overseeing a program. As such a public figure, his program is dissected by the media and scrutinized during times when fair-weather fans are jumping on and off the bandwagon. Coach Ferentz has coached his teams to Big Ten Championships, the Orange Bowl, the Rose Bowl, and many other bowl appearances, plus a most recent program-first 12-0 regular season and a trip to the Big Ten Championship game.

What sometimes goes unnoticed by the average football fan focused only on wins is that Coach Ferentz runs a program with consistent program philosophy. In sports, some teams are going to produce more success than others. At all levels, success can be based on some of the same variables that all teams experience each season including leadership, experience, chemistry, injuries, talent, and other factors. Regardless of success during the season, Coach Ferentz adheres to the core values that have guided his successful program for quite some time. He has remained consistently strong, a noteworthy example of Coach Bob Reade's definition of tradition.

As you gain more experience in coaching, your philosophy will also evolve. You will have to continue to improve your program as a coach. Each year you will look to enhance the things you were doing the year before and eliminate those things that did not work. You will also streamline your philosophy, develop better-defined program guidelines, and attempt to elevate what you were doing the year before. You will learn new drills, incorporate better schemes, and expand your knowledge of the principles of your specific sport. But your core values will remain consistent and guide that process.

Over the years, you may look back only to find your core values may have changed a little over time as well. This is not unusual because our perspectives also change as we get older. Some of the things you thought were most important when you first started out in the business may change as you get more life experience under your belt. That is part of the process of maturation.

Some coaches or organizations create what is called a mission statement, a declaration of your program goals, similar to the one below:

MISSION STATEMENT: Our program will guide student-athletes in their pursuit of excellence both in the classroom and through athletics by fostering personal qualities and attitudes that will benefit both the individual efforts and team performance now and for a lifetime.

The general idea of the mission statement can be made easier to visualize by creating specific program goals that are supported by core values and philosophy, like the examples below:

Program Goal:
Guide students to graduate with the highest GPA possible.
Core Value/Philosophy: To develop the highest GPA possible in our individuals and teams, never forget a young person's education is of the highest importance.

11

Program Goal:
Inspire a commitment to excellence.
Core Value/Philosophy: Commitment is a pillar of success in any endeavor. It will require sacrifice and discipline.

Program Goal:
Learn to work as a team.
Core Value/Philosophy: By building leaders your team will have a chance to be successful.

Program Goal:
Help individuals achieve their goals.
Core Value/Philosophy: Creating goals with timelines is critical to improved performance. Progress made toward them will help define success.

Program Goal:
Foster attitudes that transform into championship efforts.
Core Value/Philosophy: Mental and physical toughness combined with an unsurpassed work ethic will have rewards over time.

Program Goal:
Instill values that benefit team and individual performance for a lifetime.
Core Value/Philosophy: Life transcends sports. Helping to instill values and develop the personal qualities of champions will also allow individuals to make a much greater impact later in life.

LEARN FROM MENTORS, BUT BE YOURSELF

We all have role models or those whom we look up to and admire in coaching, but it is important to be who you are. It is likely you entered this profession because of the positive influence of a mentor. Conversely, you may have decided to become a coach after you experienced a coach's negative influence and became convinced that you would certainly serve as a better role model. In either case, we always look to take the things we admire from certain individuals and avoid the things we don't like in others. Take a good look around and pay attention to what your peers are doing well so you don't miss out on the opportunity to borrow many valuable ways to improve.

It is critical that you are always looking for ways to better yourself. Look for new ways to improve how you motivate. Find new ways to improve how you communicate. Discover new ways to improve how you build relationships or ways to improve how you organize, plan, or script. Becoming a successful coach includes becoming the best you can be, and that process never ends. Part of that process involves discovering new things about yourself you didn't even know existed. Some of that requires changing with the times. Great coaches are able to adjust to the changing times and find ways to better themselves and revitalize their program.

Some coaches are great at giving inspirational messages to their team, while others would experience so much anxiety they would have a difficult time being genuine because it would not fit their personality. Some coaches have a great understanding of how to communicate with officials in a positive manner while others create animosity the moment they open their mouth. There are so many skills required beyond knowledge of the game to become an effective coach that you will always have something you can improve upon for your own personal growth.

To become the best you can be, you cannot become someone you are not. Keep building upon your natural strengths and work to identify and bolster the qualities you have not managed to master yet. If you are lucky, you will have a mentor in your life who will give you an honest evaluation and point out areas where you can improve. As a head coach and now athletic director, I have always thought it is critical that I provide feedback to our coaches so they can continue to grow.

Pay attention to the things your peers are doing well and learn how and why they do them. Understand why certain things work for them, but keep in mind they may not work for you in the exact same way. Make sure to clearly recognize the areas that need improvement and differentiate them from the characteristics that need to be extinguished altogether. It is important for you to work toward continual improvement, but you should also to stay true to who you are.

Some states are well known for certain sports. When you think of Indiana you might think of basketball. Texas could be football. When it comes to Iowa, wrestling is a powerhouse. The sport's greatest competitor, Dan Gable, is an icon recognized not only in Iowa but also around the world. For high school wrestling coaches in Iowa he has been readily accessible, which cannot always be said about figureheads in other sports. I have attended clinics, seminars, open practices, camps, meets, and socials where Coach Gable has been the featured speaker.

Our school in DeWitt, Iowa, once invited him to be a keynote speaker at a reading event and he gladly obliged. One of the standing jokes in our family is the night Coach Gable called our house to confirm that he would come and speak. My wife answered the phone and Coach Gable asked if I were home.

"May I ask who is calling?" she replied, as usual.

"Dan Gable," he answered.

"Sure it is," she responded, knowing it had to be a friend impersonating Coach Gable.

"It's Dan Gable," she proclaimed in a sarcastic voice, proceeding to hand me the phone.

We were both surprised to find out it was actually Coach Gable. If you are a high school wrestling coach in Iowa, getting a phone call from him is a big deal!

One of the many things I always appreciated about Coach Gable was that his program always demonstrated core values that made his team a perennial contender. They had high program expectations, and finishing second in the Big Ten or at the NCAA tournament was not an acceptable goal. But over the years I observed the program, I noticed that Coach Gable was able to adapt as a coach without sacrificing his values. Although Iowa wrestling has always seemed to maintain certain ideals I am sure they would never sacrifice, the program has also adapted with changing times, rule changes, evolving styles, and changing attitudes of young people.

As an aspiring wrestling coach, it would have been impossible for me to try to carbon copy what Coach Gable did with his program and assume that it would work for me. Because of his unique background, skill, credibility, and knowledge, many things he did effectively would never have worked had I implemented them. Certainly there were aspects of his program I wanted to adapt to our program and characteristics I admired in him that I did attempt to emulate. But no matter how hard I try, I will never become Dan Gable and it is a waste of time to try. He is one of a kind.

But so are you. Build upon your own strengths and eliminate your weaknesses, what Coach Gable might describe as your "lesser strengths." You need to work to become the best you can be. Look around you and you will find all sorts of positive attributes you might incorporate into your own style to make it better. I've paid close attention to coaches at all levels and in all sports for the qualities that I could use to enhance my own approach. There are a lot of high-character coaches out there who are doing great things and doing them the right way.

Of course, many of my own former coaches were these kinds of mentors, who made a positive impact on me over the years. I am fortunate to have learned from the great role models of my head coaches and assistant coaches throughout my middle school years, high school programs, and college athletics. Throughout this book, I will discuss coaches I have had the privilege to learn from, who have had a great impact on me.

Some of my coaching colleagues at the high school level have also served as great mentors but are not known throughout the country. The veteran coaches I learned from were experienced Hall of Fame coaches like Pam Duncan, Neil Padgett, Jim Hetrick, and Dwight Spangler, who all had an influence on me as a young aspiring educator. If you are paying attention, you will find similar role models in your own school, coaches who are terrific leaders.

If you are fortunate, you will have a supervisor, head coach, or athletic director who will evaluate you in a discerning manner. We all want people to point out our strengths, but becoming aware of areas needing improvement will increase our chances of becoming the best we can be. Criticism may be easier to understand if it is done in a constructive manner, but how it is presented or what is being said is not as important as how we respond to it.

Just as you should want to provide your own athletes with an honest evaluation, you should also want a mentor in your life to identify areas where you can improve, someone who will be willing to say, "You can do better." Head Football Coach Mike Swider of Wheaton College, Wheaton, Ill., is one of the great men of character and integrity in our profession. He introduced me to the concept that you have to be willing to risk a relationship with your athletes and sometimes tell them, "That's not good enough!"

You should welcome someone into your life who is going to challenge you through an honest evaluation. Too many times we avoid addressing an issue, even in our personal lives, because we are worried that conversation will ruin or hinder a relationship. Being held to a high standard and knowing someone cares enough to address our shortcomings can actually strengthen our bonds and create a sense of respect. It will also make the evaluator's high expectations clear. This is not only good coaching advice, but also good advice for daily living, especially in parenting.

We know from our own experiences in athletics that teams do not necessarily grow as much when things are going well. We can become complacent and go on autopilot when we are on a roll. Failure, adversity, and challenges all serve as opportunities for growth. Although it is not fun to lose, we should always welcome a chance to get better. I did not always worry if an individual or team experienced setbacks through defeat, because it was a great opportunity to evaluate what they were doing, make necessary changes, hit the reset button and move ahead. The same is true for us as a coach. Adversity is always a chance to turn a negative into a positive and become better than we were before the loss, an acknowledgment that change is needed. Who knows if Coach Gable's drive to become an Olympic gold medalist, and his unsurpassed success as a coach, would have turned out differently had he not been inspired following the only loss of his college career, his very last match, against Larry Owings.

In 1986, the Augustana College football team I played on had a chance to break the all-time win streak record of 47 games set by the University of Oklahoma between the years of 1953-1957, while winning an unprecedented fourth straight national title. I was on the field as a senior when we unfortunately experienced a 0-0 tie in our first game of the year vs. Elmhurst College, Elmhurst, Ill. At that time, there were no tie-breaking rules, and a tie stood as a tie. Everyone was devastated, but it allowed us to take a good hard look at ourselves and reevaluate after winning the previous 36 straight. Later, Coach Reade told the media he did not think we would have won the national championship that year had we not used that early setback to refocus. We lost the record, but what we gained in the process allowed our later success.

Great coaches are able to make the most of all their opportunities, turning even failure into success.

GAME DAY

Over the years of being involved in athletics, I have seen two seemingly similar words become miles apart in terms of my definition and application. Those two words are FAN and SUPPORTER. Of course, a thesaurus would indicate that these are synonyms, but I would mostly disagree with that interpretation.

Here are the definitions:

FAN: A person who is very much interested in a sports team or entertainer and spends a lot of time watching or reading about them.
SUPPORTER: A person who approves of and encourages someone or something.

From these definitions, my observation seems to be incorrect. But the longer you are around sports, the more you will see the difference is quite striking. To me a fan is more casual in nature but often more vocal in person. Fans express a wide range of emotions and when it comes to sporting events do not hold back in their evaluations, sometimes becoming quite vocal. Fans may even give the impression they are owed something for their superficial involvement and enthusiastic loyalty. Fans can go so far as to express that they are somehow denied something basic in nature — like happiness? — if the results are not as they would have liked.

When I hear that type of fan, aka critic, geared up to point out where those doing something worthy should have done it better, I am sorely irritated. Sometimes the criticism comes from fans who have absolutely no experience or basis for the critique. They have no background knowledge and paid absolutely no price by way of time, energy, sweat, tears, or commitment to try to accomplish something worthy in that sport. They have not made a single sacrifice themselves to achieve something great or even to fail as we sometimes do. But they are typically the first to point out faults or have a solution, because in their mind the answers are always simple. We all do those sorts of things from time to time, and we do them because somehow it makes us feel a little better watching others fail, knowing we did not have the same ambition to try it for ourselves. But that is no way to live.

We sometimes talk about the concept of winning and losing in our leadership group meetings. I mention that it is important to separate who we are from what we do when pursuing our goals and dreams. Failure should not define who we are. The pursuit of excellence is certainly a worthy cause,

18

but who you really are transcends winning and losing. Winning is great, but it does not come close to replacing the potential you have for doing even greater things in your life.

Don't get me wrong, both success and failure can be an emotional roller coaster. I for one am someone who hurts when I fail and feels exhilaration when I succeed. The scoreboard, though, does not always tell the entire story of what happens. When you are defeated, you can still be disappointed, but you can also be proud. Be proud of your effort. Be proud you were a risk-taker. Be proud you took advantage of an opportunity and thankful for the opportunity you had, grateful for the experience.

I feel the same way about teams I root for as well. I love the underdog and I love rooting for a team that was down and found the heart, character, and leadership to turn things around. In the end, it is perspective that helps me understand that all the success in the world, or dealing with disappointment, does not come close to defining who I am or the impact I can have in life. It is certainly not a basis for judging others.

What the world needs, what teams need, and what all individuals need is SUPPORTERS. Optimism is a great thing. We all need someone who will always be in our corner rooting for us and give us unconditional support. That kind of support can inspire greatness. Part of that definition is encouragement. We need someone who will rally the troops when they are down. We need someone who will point out all the great qualities that develop through competition. Character development rarely comes in the thralls of victory. Struggle can often build success. Fans jump on and off the bandwagon when it is convenient for them; supporters are going down with the ship.

"Courage doesn't always roar. Sometimes courage is the little voice at the end of the day that says, I'll try again tomorrow."

—Mary Anne Radmacher

CHAPTER 1 ACTIVITIES

- What principles do you really believe in? List 3-5 core values that will help you when developing your own philosophy.

- Develop 3-5 program goals and align the core values that will help you achieve them.

- Reflect on your past and give three reasons why you want to pursue a coaching career.

- Describe a great mentor in your life who has been influential in your personal or professional development and the qualities that made that person great.

- Identify 3-5 mentors in your school or organization who can serve as a model in coaching for you.

Chapter 2

KEEP CHIPPING AWAY
Program Development

"When nothing seems to help I go and look at a stone cutter hammering away at his rock, perhaps a hundred times without as much as a crack showing in it. Yet at the hundred-and-first blow it will split in two, and I know it was not the last blow that did it, but all that had gone before."

—Jacob Riis

During the course of about 10 summers, I had an opportunity to coach on the campus of Wheaton College, Wheaton, Illinois, at the Bishop-Dullaghan Skills Camp. I really enjoyed the structure of this football camp, but one of the greatest experiences over that time was getting to know and learn from Head Coach Mike Swider. He and his staff are great coaches but also great leaders. At the camp, Coach Swider always gave to the athletes an inspirational talk which went well beyond the game of football. It was one of the reasons I wanted to have our players attend the camp. Prior to camp starting each year, the staff would attend a meeting to go over the camp schedule and expectations.

One year during his presentation, he made a statement that has resonated with me more than anything else I have ever heard in coaching: "What you see on the field is what you taught or what you tolerated."

Think about how profound and applicable that statement is to your situation. It certainly affects the evaluations we make as a coach and really can be applied to about every area of our lives. It is human nature to assign blame when the outcome of our endeavor is not as we have envisioned.

A respected leader is not afraid to take responsibility no matter how hard it is on the ego. Sometimes things happen that are out of our control. Sometimes we make mistakes.

Before you start complaining about why a player or team didn't do this or that, think about what you may have taught or what you might have tolerated. If you feel your assistant coach *should have* done something another way, *could have* done it differently, or *would have* made a better choice, take a good hard look at yourself and your methods first. There are many examples where you can apply this principle. The great thing is that it places the responsibility squarely on you.

STANDARDS FOR ATHLETES

The very first coaching lesson I ever received was from my father, Jack Kreiter. My dad was a man of few words but when he said something it usually mattered, so you had better pay attention. During my senior year of high school, my team lost a football game that we thought we should have won. In reality we were probably a middle-of-the-road team, although we thought we were far superior, at least in our own evaluation of that game.

It was a two-hour bus ride home and although I don't remember much of our conversations, I am sure that by the time the bus got back to the school that night, players had pinpointed the root of our problems — our coaches. Upon arriving home, I found my parents waiting up for me as they always did. We talked about the game and the disappointment of the loss.

At some point during our conversation I found the courage to give them the assessment that my teammates and I had come up with, making some disparaging remarks about our coaches and how they were to blame for the loss. I saw my dad pause before giving me his own evaluation. He let me know that he and my mom had been in attendance and had watched the game play out. He made it clear that as a spectator, he had not been overly impressed with my performance. He concluded by saying that for future reference, I needed to take a good hard look at myself before saying anything bad about my coaches. Otherwise, I should keep my opinions to myself. Today I cherish that lesson and always take a good hard look at myself first to see what I could have done differently to change the outcome. I still feel ashamed about the comments I made, because I had the highest respect for my coaches.

You will teach and coach your teams using examples you are familiar with. You have your own great life lessons you can use to help young people develop as players and learn about life. The longer you coach, the more insight you will gain in dealing with specific situations. Coaching won't get any easier, but your experiences will give you a wealth of information to use when handling issues.

A key to developing a solid program over time is to be consistent in the things you do. You run the risk of potential problems when you handle one situation using a certain set of guidelines and then change your policies midstream to handle another. Every situation will not be a carbon copy of the first, but consistency in your approach will help you avoid unnecessary fallout. Part of that consistency is to have a set, written, and transparent set of standards. These standards can be as broad or as specific as you would like to make them.

When creating these guidelines, keep in mind that if you generate one for every potential situation, you may end up taking a great deal of your time writing it all out, and you will still not cover them all. So creating broader-based policies may make the application more effective. For reference, lean on the handbooks of your school and your state and national guidelines. You may be given latitude to create some of your own policies specific to your program. If so, you can lean on the administration to help you develop them.

Like almost everything else, your policies may change somewhat over the long haul, based on the new knowledge you gain with experience. Whatever your set policies entail, it is important to administer them in a consistent manner. Inconsistency in application will create bigger problems as new situations arise. It may be tougher to apply certain rules to certain individuals based on their commitment level, performance, or general attitudes, but you will not gain the respect of your players, team, or community if you pick and choose when certain rules are applied to certain people. Don't surrender your values, and stand firm in your convictions.

From the onset you will be responsible for developing your policies and following through with administering them. One thing is for certain; your staff and athletes alike will be watching to see how consistently you apply your standards. By following through with discipline in a consistent manner, hard as it may be, your underclassmen will have no ambiguity as to what your expectations are. When discipline involves one of your high profile players, your other athletes will know that if you are willing to discipline that player, you will not hesitate to do the same if they themselves cross the line. Over time, consistent application of policies can create program stability as well as an atmosphere of understanding, constancy, and ultimately a level of respect.

I played college football under two very simple team rules:

1. *Obey the law.*
2. *Be a gentleman.*

Those two rules were simple and to the point. To this day I can recall them both because of their simplicity. But they also had very broad-based definitions, so that a few seemingly simple rules covered many situations. I created a more extensive set of rules in the programs I coached that included specific items covering the consequences of unexcused practices, lost equipment, or unsportsmanlike conduct.

Over the years, you will easily recognize the typical problems that the young people you coach are going to encounter, likely in regard to academics, commitment, and poor choices. Every once in a while you will have to deal with a new situation that you have never dealt with before. Having a preconceived set of policies and standards based on your governing district, state, and national rules — which are also in line with your fundamental values and philosophy — will make it easier to handle those situations when they arise.

Unfortunately, young people make mistakes. They are just like adults, who also make mistakes from time to time. For our youth, this is part of the learning process that they all go through during adolescence. Often these issues seem to them larger than life at the time, and there may be a considerable degree of emotion when their error involves consequences and discipline. Those issues are never easy for athletes, parents, and coaches to deal with. As a rule, I tried to de-escalate the emotional aspect of the issue and turn my energy to the consistent application of our standards while focusing on turning a negative situation into a learning experience. Managing your program will but much easier when you are calm and consistent.

As the saying goes, "You can never be wrong doing what's right." We all know that having high standards and consequences for our actions is a quality that we can instill in our student-athletes that will also make them better prepared for the world ahead when they encounter bigger obstacles and challenges. Through activities, they are getting a chance to shape their character under the pressure of sports before they later face more significant pressures that confront us all. Preparing for athletic competition can give them clues as to how they might prepare for a competitive world.

STANDARDS FOR COACHES

When building your staff, it is important to know their strengths and weaknesses so that you can put them in the best possible position to use their talents. It will help set up success for you, them, and the program. I once listened to a presenter at a teacher in-service meeting say that if you take a person's greatest strength and then take that same quality to the extreme, it also becomes their weakness. I have thought about that concept and applied it in my evaluations of many people, including myself. In almost all cases I have found it to be exactly true. Understanding that fine line between someone's strength and weakness is critical.

Invest quality time to look for the best possible candidates who fit your philosophy. Every coach does not have to be a clone of you, but it is critical that they treat young people the right way and are loyal to your system, so that ultimately everyone is working toward common goals. Creating a job description is a good way to clarify your expectations. Make sure they clearly understand their role and give them direction and purpose. Surround yourself with a hardworking, intuitive, and knowledgeable staff so that the information and opinions you share will be respected.

Having a variety of personalities can be helpful in providing different perspectives that may be useful when problem solving. You should welcome varying points of view, different opinions, and new ideas. After the dust has settled, though, everyone needs to be unified. Everyone, including the head coach, may have to swallow his pride from time to time when program decisions made in the interest of the team do not accommodate everyone's opinion. Remember that in the end, a head coach makes the final decisions, and all coaches should support that, even when there may be disagreement.

Be willing to delegate responsibilities and trust your assistants. Give them ownership in what you are trying to build and you will have a better chance of creating the loyalty you will need. It is easy for assistants to rally during times of success, but note which of their character traits appear during adversity. You want coaches who will stand by the program with you until the bitter end, not just when things are going well.

Confidentiality is a critical component of staff and program dynamics. People outside the program will want to be privy to insider information, so make sure you have a filter when you are out in public. If you are an assistant coach, don't talk negatively about the program outside of your coaches' meetings or "stir the pot." There are usually enough negative issues to go around during a season when coaching a team of adolescents. Keep those issues from becoming a problem.

It is advisable to always take a good hard look at yourself first before spending too much time being critical of others. One of my earliest and greatest mentors, Hall of Fame Head Football Coach Dwight Spangler used to remind his players — and was likely reminding his coaching staff, too — "You are a loser only if you act like one."

Recognize a "ship rat" ready to jump overboard, like the hypercritical common fan or someone in the community who undermines the program. It is easy to lead when things are going well, but how do you lead when times get tough? Adversity and conflict can be productive when they occur in the correct environment. Dissension will not.

As an assistant, if you are not able to be loyal to a head coach's system and philosophy, you should step aside. When you are part of a staff you should be part of the solution and not become part of the problem. If you are not willing or able to do that, remaining on staff is not fair to the person trying to build a program.

I once heard a great description of the type of coach you will want to become. Imagine yourself walking into a cafeteria and having two choices of which person you could sit next to for lunch. One choice would be to spend your lunchtime with someone who would make you feel inspired, reinvigorated, and motivated. Your other choice would be to spend your time with someone cynical, negative, and irritable. Whom would you choose to sit next to?

Become that inspiring coach and find coaches on your staff who are like-minded. You and your athletes will be spending a great deal of time around the coaches you choose. Work hard and play hard, but also develop the attitudes that mean success for yourself, your athletes, and your program.

You may build strong relationships with the people you work with and their families. You will spend a great deal of time together, but make sure you are respectful of your coaches' personal and family time. It is likely you will gain a mutual respect for the colleagues you work with, and work for, through coaching. Work hard in the achievement of your common goals and have fun in the process. Don't ever forget that you are all in this together.

If you are taking on the role of a head coach and need to assemble a coaching staff, it is imperative for you to create and administer your standards. Holding yourself to your own high standards is most important if you are going to succeed in this business as a credible leader. It is equally important that the head coach hold the other coaching staff accountable for implementing the standards. If someone on the coaching staff intends to ascend the coaching ladder and needs a recommendations to achieve those goals, whether or not they met the head coach's standards will be noted by supervising coaches.

Here is a short list of items you should consider when developing your standards.

Coaches should:
- Be great teachers and possess a positive self-image.
- Enjoy working with young people and become a positive influence on them.
- Exhibit loyalty and be honest in communication with your school, staff, and athletes.
- Model qualities such as
  how to be a winner
  how to handle losses and adversity
  sportsmanship
  leadership.
- Display the highest level of integrity and ethics.
- Know the rules, be passionate about your sport, and set tone with enthusiasm.
- Demonstrate a tremendous work ethic and take initiative.
- Be organized, and have a plan (practice, short term, long term).
- Show up on time and do more than what is required.
- Portray professionalism in being outfitted well for their duties. As they say, when you look good you also feel good.

Spend the necessary time before, during, and after the season communicating your expectations with your staff. Establish documents that clearly define your expectations for your coaches. Create written and electronic versions of these documents and make sure they have access to them. Make sure your standards are clearly defined and understood. You might even cite examples of your standards in text or at staff meetings so they can see what your standards look like in action.

It will be easy for you to evaluate the progress of your coaches if their roles and expectations are unmistakably defined and relayed to them. When a coach is not meeting your standards and you believe the coach has the ambition and potential to improve, invest the necessary time to work with that coach on making the necessary corrections. We all have had mentors who have helped us improve, and it is rewarding to see the growth in our staff members as well as in our athletes.

Head coaches cannot be afraid to have the hard conversations with their staff if warranted and your expectations and standards are not met. Make sure your conversations are confidential and stay private. You will put in many more hours than you will be compensated for, so don't do a disservice to yourself or to the program by failing to hold yourself and those around you to high standards.

Not every coach will be willing or able to meet your standards. When that happens, it is important to document the issues when they arise, noting the dates that you intervened and the results of your intervention. If something egregious occurs, make sure to address those situations immediately and keep your administration informed. Don't feel that you have to face those challenging situations alone. Use your chain of command in helping you with tough issues and staff issues.

You may feel intimidated when you first have to handle these situations, but handle them in a prompt manner. Dealing with issues as they come along may seem problematic, but it beats sitting on them for long periods of time and overlooking something that could end up becoming a bigger issue, or one that could have been corrected if addressed promptly. Make sure common sense prevails. Be firm but fair with your staff, and always handle situations discreetly and with confidentiality. Always return to your core values and philosophy when considering how to handle all situations.

If you are the head coach, work with your administrator in the evaluation of your staff. You may create your own separate evaluation process that you share with your assistants using a less formal format. Be open, honest, and transparent with your assistants and hold them accountable to your high standards. Coaching young people is a huge responsibility. Make certain your staff meets your expectations of how to treat our youth. Don't shy away from challenging your staff and point out areas in which they need improvement. Your coaches, as well as your athletes, want to be challenged and deserve your input. It is part of your obligation and responsibility to help them become the best they can be.

While attending a clinic, I listened to a successful longtime high school head coach mention that he did not hesitate to put some of his most talented, enthusiastic, and young coaches at his middle school levels. He strongly believed that building success at that level was most important for continued success throughout the entire program. Don't be afraid to move your coaches or to give them changing responsibilities. Make sure you clearly communicate to them their shifting responsibilities.

If you are the one being asked to move or change coaching assignments or responsibilities, embrace that change. Changing levels or coaching assignments only serves to better your background knowledge of the overall program, even when you are hesitant to make that move. If a supervising coach moves you to a lower level, continue to work hard. If you are making a lateral move, keep learning. If you move up, don't become complacent. Every change is a new opportunity.

Continue to evaluate yourself as a productive staff member, set new goals, and learn your position. Work hard to be a success. Your ego may take a hit if you are asked to make a move you do not fully support, but always welcome an opportunity to coach regardless of what that new position entails. Look for the long-term benefit. I made multiple moves during my coaching career and although initially I may have questioned my new role, I ultimately became a "program guy" and worked as hard as I could for my head coaches on behalf of our programs.

GAME DAY

We had always wondered what would happen if we were able to put all aspects together at once — offense, defense, special teams — and we watched that happen against a good Maquoketa team. As I was walking down to the game field Friday night, standing right in front of me was my college head coach, Bob Reade. What a big surprise! He was not there to see me, though.

First, let me say that Coach Reade is at the top of my list of coaches for whom I have the highest respect. They don't come any better than he is when it comes to coaching. He had a 50-plus game-winning streak, including multiple state championships, when he coached high school at Geneseo, Ill. Shortly after I graduated from Augustana College, where I played football for Coach Reade, he had just surpassed Knute Rockne, legendary coach at Notre Dame University, as having the highest winning percentage of any college coach at any level. Beyond his football success, though, he has always been a great role model and person. He ran a clean program and one that put football in perspective even as he gained national success. At Augustana, each player was expected to be a student first and a football player second. We were at school to get a degree and eventually contribute to society, not to play football.

Coach Reade has been elected to almost every football Hall of Fame there is, and there he was at Goodenow Field on a Friday night in Maquoketa, Iowa! He was going to watch my team play a game he had mastered. The pressure was on. Coach Reade had gotten his coaching start in Maquoketa as an assistant coach and was there for the ceremony honoring Maquoketa's 1957 undefeated team. So it gave me a lot of pride to walk off the field at half-time ahead 42-0. Not only were we were ahead by a big margin, but we looked like a product I knew Coach Reade would be proud of.

I got a chance to talk with him after the game and he mentioned that the team "really executed well." Coach Reade did not invent the "Wing T" but he certainly pioneered the type of Wing T called the Augustana Wing T or Inside Belly. He still speaks nationally about his offensive coaching philosophy, so for him to say that we "executed well"— I thought I had died and gone to heaven. There were many other things I was proud of as well, things he instilled in me that I'm sure he would have been proud of, too. We played tough football but did not cross the line and try to bring attention to ourselves with antics you regularly see on Saturday and Sunday afternoon television. We did not have personal fouls or lose our composure in a big rivalry game. We presented ourselves as a solid, disciplined football team. I was proud to see our team rise to the challenge.

In the second half we stumbled a bit, but all our players, when given a chance, kept playing and giving it their all.

A great story involving Weston Ketelsen developed during the game. He became a starter for the first time in his career Friday night and went on to have two interceptions, including one for a touchdown. He also had a deflection and three tackles. Weston had never started at any level prior to Friday, but what a great example he was of someone who continued to stay committed to our program and be an important part of it, regardless of his role. We never want our players to have their importance to our team get mixed up with whatever role they play. So I was proud to see this young man, who has stuck it out, worked hard, and continued to commit, take advantage of his opportunity in week six of his senior year and make a significant impact as a starter. Those are all things to be proud of.

Fortunately, with Coach Reade in attendance, I got the chance to highlight our football team to one of my role models and show all of the positives that our school, community, and team had to offer.

Besides, It never gets old thanking people on Monday when they say "Good game!"

"Defeat is never fatal. Victory is never final."
—Glynn James

CHAPTER 2 ACTIVITIES

- Identify a quality in your team that you would like to change that you have either taught or tolerated and how you might extinguish it.

- Described an event you have experienced in life that could serve as real life examples in helping you instill values through your program.

- Create 3-5 program guidelines or rules you would implement into your program.

- List 3-5 coaching standards that you feel are most important to you to follow as a coach.

- What are 2 things you would like to do next season that will enhance your value as a coach in your program and help you move closer to becoming the best coach you can be?

Chapter 3

BUILDING LEADERS
Developing the Athlete

"If your actions inspire others to dream more, learn more, do more and become more, you are a leader."
—John Quincy Adams

Over the years I have found it increasingly true that one of the best ways to give yourself and your team a chance to be successful is to build leaders. We have all witnessed teams that possessed a tremendous amount of skill and talent but did not become all they could be. We have also watched teams rise from the status of an underdog to win a championship. In both cases, team leadership had a lot to do with either failure or success. When a group possesses leadership and does the right things, their attitudes and efforts come together in a way that exceeds what is defined by the scoreboard. Far beyond wins and losses, there is no higher calling in our profession as a coach than to build leaders.

At some point in a coach's career, the competition will come to an end and all of our past efforts will be summarized in the record books, possibly memorialized by a few plaques hanging on our office wall, and remembered with fleeting memories of days gone by. The thrill of victory feels great but the relationships you forge with your players and staff will last longer. The experience you will have with them will be transformational.

My great-uncle and great-aunt, Carl and Esther Kreiter, used to be caretakers of a large cemetery in the Quad Cities. In my youth, I got an opportunity to work my first real job by working at that cemetery. My primary role was to push-mow around all the headstones, and there were a lot of them! The task required me to spend a lot of time walking up and down the rows of each section. Over time, I became familiar with some of the information etched in those headstones. Besides the names and dates, from time to time there would be a personal message the family wanted to include as a fitting memorial to the life their family member had lived. My guess is that within such a large cemetery there were plenty of former coaches buried there, but I don't recall any career records ever being carved on any of the headstones.

We dedicate a tremendous amount of time and energy in preparing our teams to succeed. But in the end, the legacy we leave in this profession goes well beyond our career records. We take pride in our accomplishments and pay tribute to championships with trophies, banners, and certificates. But all of us who have ever coached know that the real rewards come through the impact we make on the young people we have had a chance to spend time with.

There is nothing more gratifying in our profession than to know that as a mentor, you made a positive impact on a young person. That impact can be far-reaching and can exert a positive influence on our athletes for years to come. The ultimate tribute does not come through all the awards but at the moment one of your former athletes takes the time to say thanks for the difference you made in his or her life. When you have that happen for the first time, you will know that is what coaching is all about.

TEAM LEADERS

Competition is motivating, but the lifelong impact we make on others has the potential to influence generations of athletes. You will have your hands full preparing for practices and game plans and spending the required time to practice, break down films, and do all the other administrative duties that will require your attention as a coach. While performing all these, though, make certain you also spend time finding ways to develop leaders on your team.

As you become more experienced in your administrative duties, you will find out there are always ways to incorporate leadership development into your plans. These two concepts are not mutually exclusive. You don't have to sacrifice administrative duties to incorporate leadership development. As you work on building leaders, you will discover that building leadership qualities is a key ingredient in developing continued success in your program. One of the most critical roles a player may have on your team is that of a leader.

If you are looking for a good resource and a powerful example to illustrate the impact you can make as a leader on your athletes, teams, school, and community, let me suggest that you read *Sacred Acre*. This powerful story documents the life of Coach Ed Thomas, one of the great men and leaders of the high school ranks in Iowa football. I have used many of his leadership concepts in my own programs.

Coach Thomas was an icon around the state, not only as a football coach but also in his efforts to build leaders. His successful career in education spanned 37 years. His football programs won two state titles while producing four NFL players in the small Iowa program of Aplington-Parkersburg. But the impact he made on his players, teams, school and community surpassed even his football success.

When Parkersburg, Iowa, experienced the devastating effects of an EF5 tornado in the spring of 2008, the impact that Coach Thomas made on his community in its recovery was one of the greatest examples of pure leadership. He was instrumental in leading the recovery of the community, town, and school after the devastation of that tornado.

In DeWitt, Iowa, 147 miles east of Parkersburg, we had our annual Rent-a-Player fundraiser in the fall of 2008. During this campaign, we allowed our players to be "rented" by the residents of our community, at a cost, for fall cleanup activities the Saturday following one of our games. Each year, we would direct our donations toward some worthy cause. That year we sent our donation to the Parkersburg high school. I mention this not because we did something many others did on an even bigger scale, but because to this day I cannot tell you the results of the game the night before. I can, however, remember the satisfaction of knowing our donation went to help in the recovery of this community. Leadership is the thing that endures.

If you know the story of Coach Thomas's life, you also know it came to a tragic end. As he was leaving the school weight room one summer day, Coach Thomas was shot and killed by a former athlete dealing with personal issues. I remember getting a phone call from my wife the morning of the murder to tell me what had happened. It was a heartbreaking situation. I also remember how eerie it was, as I happened to be leaving the weight room myself that morning when I received that call. Coach Thomas, like me that morning, had been doing something that seemed so perfectly normal.

In the leadership standards we set, we want our athletes to have high expectations for themselves and to exhibit consistency in their actions. How often do we hear of players who act one way in the classroom when a substitute teacher is present and then another way during practice in front of their coaches. Or they display certain characteristics in the locker room around their teammates, but act totally different when they are away from the team with friends on the weekend. True leadership should not be situational.

I'm sure there were football strategies and X's and O's that I might have learned from Coach Thomas, but what I have incorporated the most over time were his concepts of leadership. He understood the importance of leadership to his teams and challenged his upperclassman, especially his seniors, to set high standards. He knew how critical it was for his players to develop those qualities if they were to succeed as a team. I gravitated toward that message because it is something I truly believe in.

Our athletes will likely become more effective leaders as they gain new knowledge, skills, and experience over time, but every one of our players has a leadership potential. There is not necessarily something innate, inborn, or programed into a young person's DNA that will make him ascend in a leadership role. There are concepts and principles that can be nurtured in all individuals, and I believe coaches have a great responsibility to make that a priority. Successful coaches also know that when related to performance, talent is important but leadership is critical.

The success of a team or program is reflected through its leadership, which includes both coaches and players. Develop your own leadership curriculum and teach the things you really value and believe in. Point out qualities that leaders possess and provide the tools and opportunities your participants need in order to grow as leaders. Help build athletes of high character and help them understand that they have the ability to make a positive difference in their lives as leaders. Their journey as leaders might start simply as a role they are assigned or with specific responsibilities they have in your program. This expression of leadership, though simple, may grow into something much bigger over time and far surpass the effect it had on your team or program. The opportunities to lead that you create have the potential to build lifelong leaders. These concepts may seem simple to us who occupy leadership roles but it is important that we intentionally expose our youth to concepts of leadership if we care about them becoming all they can be.

TEAM CAPTAINS

There are many different ideas about the use of team captains and how they should serve our teams. Some coaches do not use captains at all and let leadership emerge as it may. Others choose leaders from week to week or wait to announce captains until the end of the season. Some programs appoint all seniors captains. Teammates may vote for captains, or the coaches may simply assign them, based on various criteria. However it is done, the development of team leaders can make a significant impact on success during the season.

Regardless of how you assign the role of captain, it is important that you have a clearly defined purpose for that athlete. Otherwise, the role of captain may not equate to your expectations of a leader. Your captains should be more than token titled figures meeting in the middle of the field for a coin flip. You should have a vision for what their role will entail. Will they be a liaison between your staff and the players? Will they lead various aspects of practice or have a role speaking to the team? How do you involve them when discussing team issues? If you do, keep in mind that discussions involving confidential matters may not be something you want to open up to adolescents regardless of their status as a leader. At the bare minimum, have your leaders stick around with you after an event and help pick up the locker room or the bus before leaving. It is a good habit to get into, and custodians and bus drivers will recognize and really appreciate your efforts.

It is also important to remember that someone does not have to be named a captain to be a team leader. Leadership is not confined to a title. During adversity or in the heat of battle, you may see players emerge as leaders, those whom you never would have expected. You may also see players chosen to assume the role of captain may not possess the qualities essential for them to be effective or credible. Some leaders make a significant impact without being captains. Make certain to make the distinction between your leaders and your captains. You can hope those two titles will be one and the same person, but that is not necessarily true.

Team leaders can also make an impact without being a standout athlete. One of the mistakes I made over the years was failing to elevate one of our best true leaders to the position of captain because I was concerned he would not play a significant role as a performer. Early in the season it was obvious I had failed to identify our true team leader. Ineffective leadership had the potential to negatively affect our performance as well, so I quickly corrected that situation by elevating him to a leadership role. It was certainly a good lesson for me to learn.

There are many ways to go about choosing your team leaders. One of the methods that emerged over the years for me was an extensive selection process that involved interviews and introduced some real-world leadership skills for our young. The process began in the spring with the announcement that any junior or senior football player wanting to be considered a captain for the upcoming season must submit a resumé before a selected deadline.

In the meantime, to help in the process, I created an interview committee which included a faculty member, former player, assistant coach, and coach of another program. After collecting resumés, I emailed the high school faculty the names of our candidates to get their input as to what type of leader the individuals were, or were not, in the classroom. As you might anticipate, this sometimes opened up a Pandora's box!

I then set up an interview schedule and provided to our committee a list of potential questions that they were welcome to use. We often enhanced those questions with specific situations that were suggested by our faculty, including other known examples of their conduct in the school and community.

Each interviewer ranked the applicants as to known leadership qualities, resumé, and interview performance. Over the summer, I met with all the applicants and went through a leadership curriculum once a week, while continuing to monitor their roles as both vocal leaders and leaders by example during the off-season.

After our first week of practice, I used all of that data to select our leadership team. In the locker room, I posted the leadership roles, including our permanent captains. We also selected position captains to work with position coaches in the implementation of pre-practice drills that included all of the underclassmen and occurred prior to stretching while coaches were getting organized for drill periods.

I initially had a set limit of captains, but that changed over the years, which is an example of how your philosophy might change over time. I came to believe that if a young person was interested in pursuing a leadership position and possessed the qualities we were looking for in a leader, I should give that athlete an opportunity to take on a leadership role. So we expanded the number of team leaders to include all qualified candidates and utilized them in different leadership positions. When they excelled in their role, we would even rotate them on game night so they could experience the ceremonial aspect of being a captain as well.

One of the great examples of flexibility, leadership, and becoming the ultimate team player came about during our 2007 football season.

During our off-season planning, we anticipated that returning senior and outstanding player Will Maass would anchor the critical left guard position for us to effectively establish a strong running game, which had become the strength of our program. Will was an outstanding multi-sport athlete who was passionate about football. He had personal goals to play collegiate football. He was an outstanding high school player and was a returning Third Team All-State lineman.

His senior year, though, Will wanted to switch to being a running back, anticipating he would have a better chance of garnering looks from college scouts at that position, as he was a bit undersized for a lineman.

At first, we allowed Will, who was a team captain, to pursue his football goals, and he proved to be an outstanding fullback. Honestly, he would have excelled at any position because he was one of those rare high school athletes who had the right attitude and toughness to compete at a high level regardless of where he played. As it turned out, we lost the first two non-district games to start the season 0-2.

We realized that moving Will back to the offensive line had the potential of making a significant positive impact on our overall success. I was hesitant to ask Will to move back to left guard, knowing his future aspirations, but I knew what would be best for our team. I also realized his deep-rooted will to win and knew he would understand our situation.

Of course, he consented to move back to left guard and embraced the position. Not only was his performance worthy of earning him First Team All-State honors, it also propelled our team to a first-ever undefeated district title (7-2) and an eventual trip to the IHSAA 3A Quarterfinals. Lost in all our success, but never forgotten by me, was how Will exhibited the ultimate flexibility, leadership, and example of being a team player that season.

Over the years, we have had other great team leaders who sacrificed their own personal goals for the sake of team success. These examples of self-sacrifice by a young person are uniquely special and indicative of a type of leadership not often seen from young people — but critical to success.

41

LEADERSHIP GROUP

When I took on the position of our district activities director for our district in 2012, I created a leadership group that includes a junior and senior representative from each of our athletic programs. During monthly meetings we cover a regular agenda related to our athletic department as well as discussions about leadership qualities and leadership topics. Each member serves a two-year position. Prior to the holiday break our seniors identify a sophomore in their program who will replace them in the group for their own two-year term.

We have developed a document to be shared with our incoming freshmen that defines what it looks like to be an athlete in our programs. As coaches, we are always giving our players direction, through our philosophy, regarding what it takes to be successful. This philosophy may include descriptive terms that we include in our documents, meetings, or manuals. Our descriptions include concepts such as commitment, attitude, and work ethic.

Our document for freshmen includes a select set of descriptive terms that we have enhanced by providing real-life examples to use in understanding what it takes to demonstrate those qualities. For example, "What would you actually do or act like if you were 'coachable'"? One description our group used to define this concept is: "Do not make excuses. Take ownership in the learning process on your own and move forward." This document provides our young athletes with concrete examples of what our older athletes feel it takes to be a success. This document was an activity I picked up from a breakout session at our state athletic directors convention. I had some interest in the concept and felt it stood a chance to benefit our overall program. It did not take a huge effort to implement the activity, but required just a leap of faith to give it a try.

There are similar things you will try over the years that will have a continued positive influence on developing leadership, and there will be some things you try that don't reap the benefits you anticipated. In either case, it is important that you keep trying. We are always in the process of learning and there are some great ideas out there that will enhance what you are currently doing if you just care to look. You can use the old motto, "You are either getting better or you are getting worse."

The simple efforts athletes make as a leader in your school can have profound changes in school climate. You never know when a simple act will make a big difference in someone's life. At our meetings we regularly discuss the idea that "No one eats alone!" I challenge our leaders to identify students eating by themselves at school and take it upon themselves individually or as a group to sit with those students during lunch. True leadership is not about the person leading, and student-athletes may discover that small acts of leadership can have a profound effect upon them as well.

Continue to talk to your young people and challenge them to get out of their comfort zone as leaders. This might involve taking a stand against their peers from time to time. It takes courage to lead. Many of our youth worry about the personal repercussions that standing up for their values might have. I remind these leaders that those who might question or ridicule them for standing up for their convictions are likely to have an opinion they would not value or respect anyway. This is one of the real lessons that all leaders have to learn on their own.

Encourage volunteer work from your young adults. Organize community activities for your teams outside of the school. Have them participate on behalf of charitable organizations if the opportunity exists. Local food pantries will certainly need your help over the holidays.

You may also be able to find academic or athletic mentoring opportunities at the lower grade levels in your school district. For youth in your community, host a local competition of the National Football League's Punt, Pass and Kick or a similar youth activity that fits your sport. There are many things you can do in and around your school that will make a difference and help your students learn about the importance of volunteerism.

Mentoring youth is great, but you also can find activities that honor the elderly in your community. Once a year we visited our local nursing home and had our upperclassmen play bingo with the residents. When they first sat down, our student-athletes were always a little hesitant to interact with the elderly, thinking they shared nothing in common. As the night wore on, though, it was always rewarding to watch how much fun both the residents and athletes ended up having together. They eventually just relaxed and enjoyed their time doing something they may have never done on their own.

For a number of years, one of the residents playing Bingo with us was a former team captain and star player from the 1930s, Mr. Adolph Dohrmann. At the end of the night, he would always ask the guys to wheel him down to his room. They would then wait while he rummaged through a desk drawer, eventually pulling out his team photo from the 1932 undefeated team. Observing his pride as a former player and watching our players, separated by over 70 years, interact with him will always be one of my fondest memories. One year we were able to arrange an opportunity for Mr. Dohrmann to leave the nursing home and attend a portion of our game one Friday night before he passed away. As I understand it, he had an unbelievably great time.

GAME DAY

As always, it was a great feeling walking off the field at Marion last Friday night after an exciting win against a tough team. Unfortunately, I did not get to talk with all the alumni who traveled to the game, as I was waiting for a post-game interview with Mediacom.

Coach Ryan Streets mentioned that we had a lot of excited alums there. Some of the guys did stick around, and the first people I was congratulated by were Okie, Cam, and Hedrick, members of the '07 squad. It is fun not only to see this year's team so excited, but also to watch the pride in our program expressed by former players. I told our players after the game to enjoy the win, as I do with every win, but when they showed up Saturday morning it was time to get back to work. They did just that. I did notice there was a little extra enthusiasm, though, as they went through their morning workout.

I knew how tough our schedule was going to be and these guys would be tested. So far they have held up to the test. Don't forget, though, that the same kind of preparation is necessary for success in the classroom! There is an old saying, "Victory is never final. Defeat is never fatal." I was reminded of that after reading and listening to comments from two tough competitors from Friday night. In the morning I had gone online to read the article from the Cedar Rapids Gazette about our game. Drew Clark, an offensive lineman from Marion, was one of the players we had targeted as having to control if we were going to win the game. Clark is a senior and has been recruited by quite a few NCAA Division 1 programs. Over the summer, he committed to the University of Iowa. In the article, Clark mentioned that it was a tough loss, but they would rebound as a team and continue to get better as the season progressed.

Defeat is never fatal.

Another senior, one of our guys who went to battle with Clark in the trenches all Friday night long was Brock Goodall. Because of his efforts, he was one of Mediacom's Ironman Performers, along with Tyler Smith. Mediacom announcer Jerry Kiwala, broadcaster and friend of our own coach Terry Daniels, was interviewing Brock. When asked about the game, Brock mentioned that it was just a stepping-stone and that there were other teams who could also take us down, so we would have to keep working. Victory is never final.

I also found it interesting that just prior to the interview, Brock was asked what he was going to do next year. Keep in mind that Brock and the rest of our interior offensive and defensive line performed pretty well against Marion's University of Iowa recruit, Clark. Brock said that he, too, would be attending the University of Iowa next year but to study medicine.

45

The broadcaster, impressed with Brock's performance, asked Brock if the Hawkeye coaching staff had contacted him about playing football while he was there. Brock gave that kind of sideways grin that he often gives and said, "If they call me, I will."

In Brock's case, he might play next year, but football is only the here and now for the vast majority of high school players. In Brock's mind there may be next year, but there doesn't have to be. Our victory is never final because there is always another game, and our victories go well beyond the confines of football and a great game on a rainy night in Marion. Like the many alumni who traveled to watch the game, we also knew it was an awesome feeling to win a game like that. You can't duplicate that kind of feeling anywhere else. That's why we enjoy it so much, whether playing the game or watching it.

But when it's done, win or lose, there are still more hurdles to cross, more battles to fight, more victories to win.

"To achieve all that is possible,
you must attempt the impossible.
To be as much as you can be,
you must dream of being more.
Your dream is the promise of all you can become."
—Author Unknown

CHAPTER 3 ACTIVITIES

- Outline the process you would like to use in choosing team leaders.

- Describe the roles your team leaders will have relative to practice and competition.

- List 3-5 activities you could incorporate into your program in helping develop leadership on your team.

- Summarize 3 qualities that you feel are necessary for your athletes to develop, to become successful during their time in your program.

- Name a service activity you might perform in your community.

Chapter 4

REACH FOR THE STARS
The Importance of Goals

"Ah, but a man's reach should exceed his grasp, or what's a heaven for?

—Robert Browning

At our school, the concept of reaching for the stars is not a tough concept to grasp. One of our most famous graduates, Dr. David Hilmers, was a NASA astronaut and a mission specialist on four space shuttle missions, among other accomplishments in his life. He was an outstanding high school athlete and the epitome of what being a student-athlete is all about. He set his goals high in many areas of his life and maximized his potential because he was willing to pursue them. He did not limit himself because he grew up in a town of fewer than 5,000 residents in rural Iowa. I often referred to him to inspire our science students who were taking classes in the same classrooms Dr. Hilmers did at their age. Encourage your student-athletes to dream big, create a concrete vision, and pursue their goals with passion the way Dr. Hilmers did.

Many coaches love using quotes. I am one of them. Written words can be a source of inspiration for us; inspiring passages make us think.

Our athletes desire to be motivated, too; motivation urges us to act. I'm not sure who wrote the motivational words "Practice makes perfect," but I do know Vince Lombardi got it right when he once said, "Practice does not make perfect. Only perfect practice makes perfect." Practice also makes permanent, so make sure you are doing things the right way at practice. It is critical to success. Concepts like these, disseminated by way of a motivational quote, can be important tools in getting your athletes to think about creating good habits and eliminating bad habits during training.

Practicing something incorrectly will create something permanent, but unfortunately it will lead to bad habits. Getting your athletes to do things right is what we are after. The habits they develop in practice will certainly be the same as what you will witness during competition.

Someone once said that on the road to success you can be sure of one thing: No one will be there to cheer you on when you go the extra mile. You, however, are rare person in your athlete's life who will be there to inspire and motivate them as you cheer them on along their journey when they dream big. Go the extra mile!

In reality, you are going to be a significant source of inspiration and motivation to your athletes, but if they really want to achieve something big, they are going to have to overcome many of life's obstacles by themselves.

Throughout my life, I have used a quote that I once read while I was recovering from cancer as a 17-year-old. It has been a source of inspiration to me and motivated me when facing adversity. I still have this quote positioned over my desk.

"Most men quit when they begin to tire.
Good men go until they think they are going to collapse.
But the very best know that the mind tires before the body
and push themselves further and further, beyond all limits.
Only when these limits are shattered
can the unattainable be reached."
—Dr. Mark Mysnyk

SETTING GOALS

Setting goals is an essential process in the development of our athletes, teams, and programs. Goals are also important in our professional and personal pursuits as well. Someone once told me that by doing something as simple as writing down your goals you will have increased your chance of accomplishing them by 110 percent. I have looked at various resources and cannot find any hard data that indicates 110 percent, but research consistently will show that you increase the chance of achieving your goals by doing something as simple as writing them down on paper.

When you first sit your athletes down and do goal-setting activities, be prepared for them to unknowingly exclude the concrete goals that will be necessary for them in their pursuits as they thoughtfully write down their visions and dreams, such as: *I want to win a State Championship. I will be an All-Conference player. I want to become the most inspirational athlete our school has ever produced.* There is nothing wrong with having a vision or dream, but these are future expectations or guiding passions, not concrete goals. In contrast, goals provide the detailed roadmap necessary to reach your destination, your visions and dreams. You will want to redirect athletes and help educate them on writing goals, using the many resources out there to assist you in this process. Goals involve a timeline. Goals require sacrifice. Goals will be measurable. Goals will necessitate verifiable progress.

Ralph Waldo Emerson once wrote, "Life is a journey, not a destination." Goals, dreams, and visions can be related to that. The destination is your vision and dream, while your goals are the journey it takes to get there. A vision is your guiding light that will help keep you on the correct path while you are taking the necessary steps toward it. Goals are those steps you take.

Goals are necessary to keep athletes making progress toward their destination. They are checkpoints along the journey of success. If their timeline is not met, athletes can re-evaluate or rewrite their goals. The achievement or failure to reach our goals is sometimes used by individuals to describe their success or lack of it, but it is important for all of us to understand we are not defined by our goals. This is where perspective in sports may be necessary. Goal setting is essential prior to the pursuit of achievement, but that quest does not represent who you actually are.

Coaches and athletes can be hard-core competitors and become fixated on pursuit of victory. In reality, much of our effort is preparation for bigger things in life to come. The heartache we feel from adversity will serve only to strengthen our character, just as triumph in victory will teach us how to handle success. We might accomplish great things through competition and receive marvelous accolades for our achievements, but these will pale in comparison with what we will be able to achieve outside the realm of athletics. Athletics becomes an important part of life, but always remember we were made for bigger and better things in life.

Winning and losing are end results and not our goals. Our focus then should be on our preparation and not on the final product. If you develop winning attitudes and learn to give successful efforts, you will likewise improve your chance of winning.

There are many aspects that affect the final score of a contest. Items like conditioning, skill, strategy, experience, strength, speed, and nutrition all play a part in the final outcome. Goals may help you improve each of those areas but a focus on winning does not address deficits in any of them. Control your controllable, and invest your time and energy into things that will make a difference in performance.

Effort and attitude are also vital qualities necessary for success outside athletics. As we know, there will be many opportunities for our young people to start heading down the wrong path every step of the way. Coaches, through our platform of athletics, can serve as the positive influence to help keep them on the right path. Inspire young people to use their moral compass and develop honest values.

Regularly preach a drug-free lifestyle, along with making good choices in their lives, and urge them to surround themselves with people who will help them achieve their goals. Motivate them to stay focused during their pursuit. Reaching that destination requires goals but it also requires commitment, sacrifice, and self-discipline. It necessitates that they believe in themselves. Be the person in their lives who helps build up their self-esteem to keep them on the right path.

On the following three pages are goal-setting sheets I developed that you can tailor for your particular sport and culture to build a relationship with your athletes and to help them achieve. Use items that go beyond skill development and performance to help your athletes develop winning attitudes, grow as leaders, and become productive citizens. Spend time in the off-season to discuss their goals.

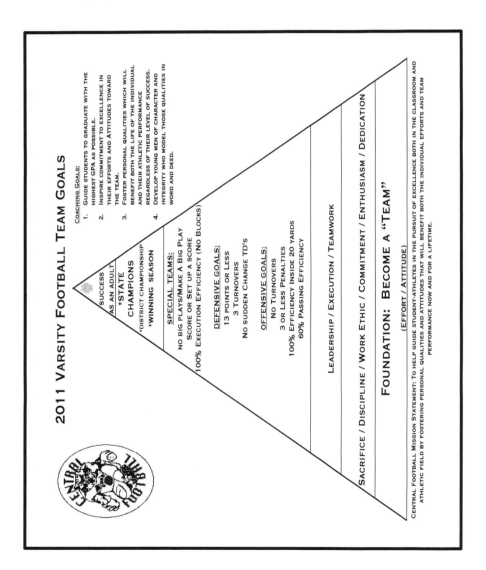

2011 VARSITY FOOTBALL TEAM GOALS

SUCCESS AS AN ADULT

*STATE CHAMPIONS

*DISTRICT CHAMPIONSHIP
*WINNING SEASON

SPECIAL TEAMS:
NO BIG PLAYS/MAKE A BIG PLAY
SCORE OR SET UP A SCORE
100% EXECUTION EFFICIENCY (NO BLOCKS)

DEFENSIVE GOALS:
13 POINTS OR LESS
3 TURNOVERS
NO SUDDEN CHANGE TD'S

OFFENSIVE GOALS:
NO TURNOVERS
3 OR LESS PENALTIES
100% EFFICIENCY INSIDE 20 YARDS
60% PASSING EFFICIENCY

LEADERSHIP / EXECUTION / TEAMWORK

SACRIFICE / DISCIPLINE / WORK ETHIC / COMMITMENT / ENTHUSIASM / DEDICATION

FOUNDATION: BECOME A "TEAM"

(EFFORT / ATTITUDE)

COACHING GOALS:
1. GUIDE STUDENTS TO GRADUATE WITH THE HIGHEST GPA AS POSSIBLE.
2. INSPIRE COMMITMENT TO EXCELLENCE IN THEIR EFFORTS AND ATTITUDES TOWARD THE TEAM.
3. FOSTER PERSONAL QUALITIES WHICH WILL BENEFIT BOTH THE LIFE OF THE INDIVIDUAL AND THEIR ATHLETIC PERFORMANCE REGARDLESS OF THEIR LEVEL OF SUCCESS.
4. DEVELOP YOUNG MEN OF CHARACTER AND INTEGRITY WHO MODEL THOSE QUALITIES IN WORD AND DEED.

CENTRAL FOOTBALL MISSION STATEMENT: TO HELP GUIDE STUDENT-ATHLETES IN THE PURSUIT OF EXCELLENCE BOTH IN THE CLASSROOM AND ATHLETIC FIELD BY FOSTERING PERSONAL QUALITIES AND ATTITUDES THAT WILL BENEFIT BOTH THE INDIVIDUAL EFFORTS AND TEAM PERFORMANCE NOW AND FOR A LIFETIME.

Central Football Athlete Evaluation Sheet

NAME_____ GRADE:_____ AGE:_____ PARENTS NAME:_____

Defensive Position:_____ Cell Phone #:_____

Offensive Position:_____ Email:_____

	2009 August	2010 March	2010 August	2011 March	2011 August	2012 March
Height	—	—	—	—	—	—
Weight	—	—	—	—	—	—
Bench Max	—	—	—	—	—	—
Vertical Jump	—	—	—	—	—	—
Clean Max	—	—	—	—	—	—
10 Yd. Dash	—	—	—	—	—	—
40 Yd. Dash	—	—	—	—	—	—
Agility Run	—	—	—	—	—	—
12-Minute Test	—	—	—	—	—	—
Total Score	—	—	—	—	—	—

	Self Evaluation	Coaches Evaluation
Mental Toughness	1 2 3 4 5	1 2 3 4 5
Coachability	1 2 3 4 5	1 2 3 4 5
Strength	1 2 3 4 5	1 2 3 4 5
Technique	1 2 3 4 5	1 2 3 4 5

Team Goals _____

Individual Goals _____

Academic Goals _____

Weight Room Goals _____

Better Person Goals _____

FB / Career Dream _____

53

2008-09 Central Wrestling Goal Sheet
Name:

Individual Goals:

1. Be willing to dream. Attack your vision! Know your goals!
2. Understand your obstacles but don't destroy your motivation.
3. Set your own goals. Be responsible for the progress. Include a timeline.
4. Surround yourself with the people who believe in you and will help you achieve.
5. Set realistic goals for your skill level. Unrealistic goals will almost guarantee failure.

Long Range Goal
(Timeline:)

1.

Long Range Goal
(Timeline:)

1.

Personal Goal
(Timeline:)

1.

Short Range Goal
(Timeline:)

1.

2.

Short Range Goal
(Timeline:)

1.

2.

Pillars of Success

_____

_____

Practice Goal

1.

2.

Practice Goal

1.

2.

Examples:
Courage, Commitment,
Confidence, Discipline,
Effort, Attitude,
Motivation, Work Ethic

Scholastic Goals: _____

(D/F Class & Teacher): _____

Team Goals: _____

Rate your commitment level to wrestling: 1   2   3   4   5
                                                 (Low)   (High)

Why are your strengths?

What is your biggest "roadblock" to reaching your goals at this time?

Questions or comments to coach:

54

Build a positive relationship with your athletes to ultimately affect individual performance and team success. On the third sheet, what I call Pillars of Success are the core values I asked our athletes to identify as helpful in directing their success.

For me, these pillars represent core values of attitude and effort. For another person they might represent determination and respect. These pillars are the foundation that will help athletes stay committed to their goals.

Building a positive relationship with your athletes can be an important step in helping them achieve their goals. There are many reasons why these relationships are such an important aspect of achievement. We all have had a coach who was both inspirational and motivating. That coach may be the reason you coach today.

My guess is that you do not remember many of the specific strategies that person prescribed or most of the individual conversations, but you do remember how that coach made you feel. If your relationship was a positive one, you can have a life-changing opportunity to help them pursue success. The emotional and personal aspect of sports is important and in the end, one of the things best remembered.

PERSONAL STORY

If you get the opportunity to coach your own children, you may find that it is both a wonderful experience and a potentially challenging one. Your own kids will likely not be that much different from any of your other athletes except in the depth of your relationship with them. For me, that opportunity was something very special, but it did get tricky at times. I was always fortunate to have great assistant coaches who took on additional roles as communicator when negotiations between my son, Casey, and me broke down. I did not get a chance to directly coach our daughter, Haley, but she was one of the outstanding students I had a chance to teach, and I know along the way she picked up a few lessons as a coach's kid that gave her a perspective on sports that was a little different from that of her peers.

Of all the things Casey really responded to over the years, goal setting was the most influential. My wife, Jenny, and I witnessed firsthand the influence and importance of goals during the course of his career. At the end of his freshman year in high school, he created a poster full of goals and hung it over his bed at home. It was handwritten and included goals for each of his sports as well as training goals, academic goals, and leadership goals.

He was a four-sport athlete and when my wife and I read his poster, we noticed he had set some lofty goals for himself in each area. We honestly thought maybe he had bitten off more that he could chew, but in the spirit of dreams, visions, and goals, we did not comment on them. These were his goals, not ours. Our role would be to provide a support system for him. That poster remained above his bed for the next three years.

As we took a closer look at that poster upon his graduation, it was interesting to see just how many of the goals and dreams he had actually achieved. He had not realized all of them, but it was impressive to see what his hard work, discipline, and drive had done for him. His goals had given him some direction in making the most of his opportunities.

He was not highly recruited by many Division I schools during high school. The University of Iowa offered him an opportunity to attend school as a walk-on football player, and after some deliberation, he chose to continue his career there. He would later say the reason he chose the Hawkeyes was that he wanted to see how good a player he could become, and he felt their program gave him that chance.

After the home college football games, we would meet in his apartment for dinner and some family time. Often we would hang out in his bedroom after eating and talk, while his teammates and their families occupied other parts of the apartment. At some point during his freshman year, over his bed appeared a new list of goals he had set for himself, this time typed. It was not a large poster like the one he had written in high school, but the content was similar. He had included the next level of goals for himself covering areas of training, leadership, academics, and performance. He now had NFL aspirations. Once more we silently questioned some of these lofty goals, but we knew our role. Again, after his five years at Iowa, he had achieved many of the goals and dreams he had set for himself.

In the spring of his senior year, he signed a free-agent contract with the Dallas Cowboys. Using technology, we got a chance to talk to him from time to time while he was participating in rookie mini- camp. One evening while we were Skyping, I noticed that positioned behind him, taped above the bed in his apartment, was a new set of goals. I could not read them, but I was sure I knew the content. Goals helped him direct his actions toward his vision.

To our athletes, though, we need to stress that success is not really as simple as merely establishing goals. Even though we write down our goals, good things will not automatically happen. As important as those words on a piece of paper are, they cannot replace the effort and attitude it takes to achieve them. Anyone can write a vision or a goal on a piece of paper, but to have the belief, discipline, self-sacrifice, work ethic, and fortitude to follow through and pursue them is an altogether different story. Casey, like everyone else, has faced his fair share of tough times and adversity along the way and will face more challenges ahead, but by setting goals he set himself up for achievement.

We coaches need to be a support system for our athletes. We need to be there for them when their emotions may tell them it is time to quit or they think they have done all they can do. We need to inspire, motivate, and challenge them when we see them developing self-destructive attitudes that will surely lead to failure. Help direct them down the path of success through your knowledge, experience, and encouragement.

It is equally important to be there and pick them up when they get knocked down. It is okay to break away from the old stereotype of a stern, uncompromising, and hard-hearted coach. Setting standards, holding them accountable, and pushing them to their limits will help them learn valuable life skills necessary to be successful, but showing them compassion will teach them the importance of empathy and understanding. Both are invaluable in building strong relationships between coaches and athletes.

GAME DAY

While attending church service, I was chatting with Coach Terry Daniels and I happened to notice Nate Keeney in front of us with his new stylish haircut. I then noticed he was wearing a playoff T-shirt from 2003 with the team roster on the back. My thoughts wondered off to some great memories from that year. I was reliving the playoff game vs. Waukon and thinking about Steven Jeffers blocking an extra point, which later was the difference in the game. There was a big interception by Mitch Lincoln and an important return by Ryan Leuer. I could see Kale Petersen hooking up with Austin Curtis for a critical first down and our workhorse Tyler Driscoll icing the game behind Andrew Goodall and Josh Wold... great memories. Suddenly I was alerted as I heard these words from the scripture reading — "turning away from listening to the truth and wander off into myths." This was a sign I should be paying attention.

As I listened on, I heard words like "be sober-minded, endure suffering" and later, "DON'T GIVE UP." The context was not meant to stimulate thoughts of football, but that's what I was thinking, and I thought to myself what a great phrase to describe those seniors. On Senior Night, the seniors, along with our juniors, were able to become the first-ever district champions at Central. When I look back at some of the things this group endured, "don't give up" is fitting.

Until last year this group had never experienced a winning season in football. They had developed a reputation as a bunch of renegade individuals who were not a cohesive, coachable group. When I daydream in church ten years from now, one thing that I will always remember about this group is the example of TEAM that has emerged. How hard they have worked and how easy it has been to be around them. Many of our seniors have made it a priority to build relationships with our juniors and thus make this a "team."

Dylan Azinger was not even going to play football but became an All-State player. Kale Holst did not go out until he was a sophomore but made a big difference in the success of our team. It appeared that one of the premier young athletes, Jesse Pennock, was never going to be able to play again after an injury his freshman year, but he overcame physical adversity to become an outstanding player. Seth Garton was a backup at QB and a little shaky at best but developed into a highly respected quarterback and leader for us. Coach Kevin Roling paid a personal visit to Seb Meggers' house to get him to come in and pick up his equipment; Seb played a vital role on the team. Andrew Akers had previously given football a try and decided no thanks, but decided to go out this year, and played well for us. There are other individual testimonies; these are some who come to my mind as I think about our win

Friday night.

DON'T GIVE UP — a great motto for this season, one used by our guys after 2-for-2 losses at the beginning of the season. Congratulations to this group, you're committed, so you've put man's greatest strength behind you. You have sacrificed, so you deserve success and you've gone out and earned it! Remember, we want to finish strong.

> *"... and so they set sail for the Land of Possibility*
> *where anything could happen, and often did."*
> —Unknown

CHAPTER 4 ACTIVITIES

- Write an inspirational and motivational quote that has made you both think and act during your career.

- What vision do you have for your coaching career?

- List 3-5 goals, including timelines, which will help you in your pursuit to attain your dream.

- Name a coach who was instrumental during your career as an inspirational and/or motivational supporter and what influence that coach had on you.

- Develop a goal-setting sheet for individual athletes or your team in your program.

Chapter 5

FEEL LIKE A CHAMPION
Developing Winners

"Winning is not a sometime thing; it's an all-the-time thing. You don't win once in a while; you don't do things right once in a while; you do them right all the time. Winning is a habit."
—Vince Lombardi

I recently had a nice conversation with one of our former athletes who is now a school administrator. As with most similar conversations, we were reminiscing about the good old days. He had been blessed with talent, but he wrestled in the early days when we were still working to build a competitive program. Although he had experienced some success, he had not had the luxury of participating in an established, mature program. Standing nearby was another former athlete who wrestled at about the same weight class but about 15 years later. He had benefited from a more established program and experienced a great deal of success at the state level.

I made sure to introduce these two former wrestlers to each other, and I let both know how important their commitments were to our program and how I appreciated both of them. I also made certain that our more recent graduate recognized that the success he experienced had a lot to do with the foundation that was established by those earlier athletes who did not have those same opportunities. We want our athletes to develop a sense of pride in their program, regardless of whether the program was in its early stages or operating at peak level.

GIVE YOUR BEST EFFORTS

Take pride in your program history and value all of those who have come before and done things the right way. Our society is in need of people who will help young people develop a sense of commitment. Commitment, along with all the other great qualities developed while participating in sports, will serve our athletes well when they pursue future endeavors. The impact you can have on your athletes is far-reaching, so be ever mindful of how you approach your craft.

Early in my coaching career, someone once told me, "Don't complain about your athletes because they are the only ones you have!" The athletes who report on Day One of practice are the same athletes who will be working to implement your strategies and help you to achieve your own program goals. I often have told my coaches when your hopes and dreams are in the hands of a bunch of 17-year-olds, things are not always going to go as planned. One of the crazy aspects of this profession is that our happiness is sometimes tied to the performance of a bunch of adolescents.

You may not always have the amount of talent you had hoped for each and every year. When you begin working on building champions, you can't change your reality by hoping for a different group of athletes, a better set of skills, or improved attitudes. Make the most of your opportunities and press forward. Focus on making a difference with each group you have, and you will develop a sense of self-satisfaction. Surge ahead with blinders on and be as productive as you can regardless of your circumstances. Give all your athletes all your best efforts.

Coach Dwight Spangler used to mention when developing a new, less talented, or inexperienced group that "The future is now!" He made sure his staff understood that it was not fair to our seniors to approach it any other way. By declaring through word or deed that you are "building for the future," you sell your current athletes short. The athletes who show up with enthusiasm and make the commitments to do things the right way deserve your best efforts, even when things don't go your way in competition.

As coaches, we know that we sometimes do our best job of coaching and work our hardest during a season when we did not necessarily have a lot of success on the scoreboard. Because our critics sometimes look only to results when valuing achievement, they overlook all the other positive efforts that went on during the season which are not reflected in wins and losses. It may be difficult at times, but don't let your disappointment and frustration direct your actions. It is only fair that you continue to strive for excellence even through tough times. Those are the times when you will reveal your true character.

A good highlight film can make a miserable season look like a fairly successful one. You might have to consider showing one when creating closure at your end-of-the-year banquet. There is always a way to find positives when reflecting on your season. Regardless of how abysmal the results were, you can always look for something encouraging that you can build upon. Find the silver lining.

Learn as much as you can by studying other successful programs, but don't wish you were somewhere else. Make the most of the opportunities you have in front of you. Set your goals high, but don't covet other programs when you have a chance to do something special where you are.

My longtime assistant wrestling coach, Darol Snyder, used to use a fishing analogy regarding this. If you have ever done any fishing you will understand that when you are fishing in one location, you often look to another part of the lake wondering if the fishing would be just a little better over there. Likewise, people fishing in that location may be looking at where you are, thinking the same thing.

We sometimes think the best situation is someplace else and fail to realize what we have in front of us. I have shared this concept with college football recruiters who sometimes overlook local talent, anticipating they might find something better halfway across the country.

Likewise, you should always be looking for ways to improve, even when things are going well. In your search to make the necessary changes, remember honesty is the best policy. Facing or expressing the brutal truth will be necessary from time to time. Sugarcoating a problem area making a negative impact on your individuals, teams, and programs will not help to address the changes that are needed. Sometimes the truth hurts. You can always find a way to justify what you do, but you will be reluctant to experience much growth that way.

Building a winning program will take patience and it may take some time. Do things the right way, and you will start to see the results of your hard work and positive attitude over time. Coaching can be a thankless job; don't expect a lot of pats on the back when you start turning things around. There may be many expectations and opinions regarding the job you do, but not too many thanks for going above and beyond. Regardless, keep building a sturdy foundation.

In the early '90s, our wrestling program was starting to get a little better and our numbers were increasing. My brother, Eugene, was coaching with me at the time, and we had worked hard to convince new athletes to give wrestling a try while doing some creative things at practice to keep them interested.

We were participating in a triangular meet with some neighboring schools and got a chance to watch the other two programs compete before we wrestled either of them. After watching both teams, we were certain we had the manpower to win both dual meets, which had not happened often in recent years. As it turned out, we were soundly defeated by both teams.

Eugene and I were disappointed, and after getting the boys on the bus we "let them have it" with a most inspiring speech. We decided to challenge them by offering an optional practice the next day, which we wanted only those who were the most committed and motivated to attend.

If not, they could take the night off and stay home. We were convinced our inspirational message resonated with all of them and would certainly turn them into winners by morning, with all wrestlers ready for a new challenge.

The next day we opened up the doors to the wrestling room anticipating a group of hungry, motivated young athletes. What we found instead was a lone wrestler.

We made a decision that afternoon that all the coaxing and encouraging was producing big numbers but was not producing the outcome we had worked for. We reevaluated what we were doing and decided the athletes around whom we wanted to build our program needed to be challenged with an increased intensity. From that point on, we worked hard to create a challenging atmosphere and not to appease the masses. It allowed our program to take another step forward.

BE THAT COACH

There is not a better time in history for us to be a positive influence on young people. Be the coach who gives your best every day regardless of whether things are good or bad, and be the coach who models great character and integrity during both extremes. Provide honest feedback in a productive manner and don't leave your athletes emotionally stranded.

Athletes merit your best effort, but they will also need your criticism and discipline. They deserve a challenging environment, too. Few young people are going to directly ask you for these things, so you will need to make it a priority to build them into your program. Create a structured atmosphere where the expectations are high and clearly defined. Develop practice intensity and push your athletes to levels they may not believe they can reach. Done right, this approach will help them build the self-confidence they will need in their abilities. When you gain the trust and respect of your athletes, you can get them to believe and achieve even more than they initially thought was possible.

Help your athletes learn to persevere and help them believe they can. We all like a little latitude, freedom, and independence from time to time, but an unstructured, laissez-faire approach to training will not be conducive to success. An understanding of your specific sport, combined with the individual personalities you have on your team, may dictate what modifications you will need to make in your basic approach. You may be a bit more unconventional and creative in your methods, but the framework of your program structure should be well thought out.

When criticizing your athletes, focus on the individual's technique or performance and not on the person. Don't make conversations personal, and do not use belittling or condescending language. If you are addressing a poor attitude or poor choices, you may have to challenge them directly, but you can do that without making it a personal attack. Nothing is more repulsive than coaches who tend to the needs of their athletes only when things are going well and abandon them during adversity. Athletes see through that kind of pettiness. There is absolutely no place for any coach to demean or humiliate an athlete. It is a sure way for our athletes to lose respect for their coach and see any relationship with their coach as meaningless.

You are the adult with lots of life experience and maybe someone who has already gone through trial by fire to help you get where you are. These are young adults who may not have it all figured out yet.

As a classroom teacher, I had minimal issues with classroom discipline because I kept that one simple fact in mind when disciplining students who had misbehaved. I was an adult and they were young, naïve kids. I did not take personally the things they might have said or done, even if directed toward me. Just as we do in our own lives from time to time, students express their frustrations as anger that often has nothing to do with a specific situation. There may be more complex issues involved in their personal lives.

When addressing poor choices, address them quickly. Be firm and be consistent. Be fair in your evaluations, but be understanding and sensitive to their developmental age. Is their poor choice age appropriate? As disappointed as we are, a poor choice is sometimes an unfortunate part of adolescent development. It does not make the situation right or acceptable, but it is also not the first or last time a young person will make that kind of mistake. Many of us have gone through those experiences ourselves. What is most important for future success is to get to the root of the problem and turn a negative situation into one that they can respond to and recover from, becoming strengthened in character in the end.

We all have had players we perceived as not giving their best efforts. Those below-par efforts or lack of focus, discipline, or desire may have led to poor choices during an event. Work to find an angle that will help inspire greatness and help them overcome those deficits to become all they can be both physically and emotionally.

Help them understand that championship efforts start with good attitude. Without it, the pursuit of goals in life is futile. Whether or not they ever become exceptional players, you should always strive to develop exceptional people of high character. Most of us don't have the self-discipline to make the changes we need to make, or often to do the things we need to do for ourselves. Coaches serve a vital role in providing the structured setting that individuals will need in order to excel. Everyone on Planet Earth has just one thing that is exactly the same as the next person's… 24 hours in a day. What we choose to do with that time will make a significant impact on our lives. Our attitude is likely the quality that will guide those choices. Making good choices is a big part of that self-discipline.

I used to listen to a motivational cassette tape, which was a series of lectures by classic coaches. It included speeches by Lou Holtz, Johnny Majors, Joe Paterno, and others. I found it inspirational and I used to play it over and over trying to pick up on something new that I could apply to our programs. Coach Paterno mentioned that he never wanted his athletes ever to question that he was not aware how badly they wanted to be successful. As a coach, I have reflected on that statement many times. Whether our players possess a great amount of talent or are still in the developing stage, I refer to that concept when attempting to provide opportunities for our athletes. I never want them to think I short-changed them because I didn't realize how good they wanted to be.

All of our athletes should feel as if they have been given a chance to succeed. I use the word succeed, because success is not going to look the same for everyone. All individuals possess different levels of physical skills, and we all develop at a different pace. When you include all the variations in commitment level, skill set, focus, drive, and all the other qualities an athlete needs to excel, it confirms that all of our athletes are going to be different.

Sometimes physical development occurs early, sometimes late. Sometimes we have athletes who are totally gifted but have deficits in the area of attitude or effort. These are the ones who may demand a great deal of our time. We also have those who are models of great attitude and always give superior effort but were not blessed with a competitive bone in their body, or they weren't blessed with the physical attributes it takes to perform at a high level in their sport. These are the ones who are going to be a success later in life even though all their great personal qualities may not correlate to success in the sport you are coaching. Occasionally, we have an athlete who has a rare combination of attitude, effort, and the physical skills to match. These individuals have the chance to be great.

Regardless of what category the athlete fits into, and all the other categories in between, each one deserves to feel valued in your program. I had success with valuing athletes of all ability levels because I made a conscious choice to make that a focus of my coaching philosophy.

The best example of that was Levi Spain, a young man I really enjoyed coaching. Levi was home-schooled but approached me late in high school, wondering if he could participate in our football program. Our school district had parameters to allow that to occur, and I always welcomed interested athletes. Levi had a tremendous attitude but had never participated in organized football and was well behind his peers in skill development. We had a competitive team at the time so he did not see much action other than a few appearances on special teams and more significant playing time during junior varsity games. He was a real asset at practice on our scout team and often earned weekly recognition by staff and teammates for his efforts.

Levi never started a game for us at the varsity level, but after the season he asked me what my thoughts were about extending his playing days and trying to play at the college level. My first thought was, *Try?* You had better do more than try if you are going to make a commitment at that level. My second thought was, *This is what our program is all about!* We had not extinguished Levi's vision or motivation based on playing time or his status as a starter. He felt valued and had the confidence to set even bigger goals for himself.

In the end, my advice was that I would hate for him not to take advantage of an opportunity and then years later have regrets that he had not pursued it. I was a 100 percent supporter of his goal, and I let him know I would talk to any coach on his behalf. Levi was a good student so acceptance into a college was not an issue. When he made the choice of a good Division III school in Iowa, I had some connection with that coach and made the call.

The coach was an exceptional person and outstanding coach. The school had great tradition and facilities and was a competitive Division III program. They also did not cut athletes from their program. I was honest in my evaluation of Levi and my expectations of how he might fit in at the collegiate level. We have had a number of athletes go on to play college football at all levels over the years, and I played college football myself, so I had some background knowledge as to what it would take and how Levi might do.

Many of our former players discovered the commitment level required to be successful at the next level did not match their desire to play. Levi was definitely a young man of conviction but I honestly was not sure if he would survive the experience in that intense environment. In the end, he played for his entire four-year career. To this day he can live without regret and take pride in the fact that he pursued his vision with passion.

Levi's success is one of the great stories about a player in our program, and I am so proud of him. It is a great illustration of how the approach in our program was successful in helping to build young men.

Through the years of coaching, something special may happen to you, which will have the same impact on you that you have attempted to make on your athletes. You will be filled with pride as your players return after becoming a success in life. You will not see all of them directly, but you will hear from time to time what they are doing or how they are doing and it will make you proud. There will be some you will stay in contact with over the years.

Since 2003, All-State offensive lineman Andrew Goodall still calls me the night before football games to check in and see how things are going. It is always special to talk to him but also to watch what he has done with his engineering degree, which has included making a difference in protecting the citizens of New Orleans since Katrina devastated their communities in 2005. It is great to stay in touch with him and watch his family grow.

Via the Internet, I have also had the chance to keep up with a former foreign exchange wrestler, Nyamtsogt Ganbold of Mongolia. It was a lot of fun getting to know him and introducing him to a sport he had never experienced before attending our school. Those were great times and staying in touch with him halfway around world is unique. He was back in the United States for a judo competition a few years ago and drove from Chicago one afternoon to say hello, and I recently got the chance to help him edit his doctoral thesis.

Your athletes are going to come back as proud military members, lawyers, teachers, minsters, laborers, and alternative professions and situations that will make you proud. From time to time you may even start your own coaching tree, as they get involved in our profession. If you coach long enough, what your athletes do for a career will cover the gamut of professions. They will have become great spouses and parents and will be making significant contributions in their own communities, sometimes moving back to their hometown.

Unfortunately, as you get close to those you coach, you will have to watch them or their families experience heartbreaking situations. One of the first athletes I built a close relationship with passed away in a tragic car accident. Another great young man I got close to was taken away far too soon by a rare medical condition. There have been others lost to tragic situations much too early in life.

You never know what you will have to face in life, but unfortunately, adversity is a given. It is one of the reasons why it is important to make the most of your time together. You can make a significant impact on their lives. You'll never regret it, and they will never forget it.

You will end up celebrating great things in their life as well. You will attend weddings and get introduced to the next generation when they have their own children. If you stay in one place long enough, you might teach or coach a second generation. Their successes and your pride in them will not have a thing to do with any of the accolades they did or did not receive as a player.

When you coach, you have an exciting and important opportunity and responsibility to make an impact during your time together. With every coaching opportunity, you have a chance to affect upcoming generations through your mentorship.

I could go on and on about all of the athletes I coached, as each one was special. I am as proud of them now as I was then.

CREATE THE CULTURE OF INTEGRITY

We hear the word culture thrown around when it comes to athletic programs. The culture that exists may be classified as good, bad, or in need of major repair. Master architects seem to have a knack for creating the good culture that others try to emulate. We work hard to change a culture that needs to be repaired because it hinders our performance. It seems to be a concept of vital importance if you are going to have a successful program. What is your culture?

To me, culture is the personality of your program. It is a complex interaction of quite a few different elements. It includes the attitudes and values that are pervasive throughout your program. They seem to be linked to a coach's philosophy, standards, and organizational structure.

Culture is an expression of beliefs that a group stands for, and it appears to influence the actions of those involved. However it is defined, it is quite certain that head coaches have a major influence on creating culture and promoting it through a shared vision.

There is a hierarchy to sports programs. The head coach is responsible for communicating with superiors and following district policies while developing a philosophy based on his or her vision. A head coach disseminates that program to assistants or to coordinators if the staff structure has those dynamics. If you are an assistant coach, you will implement that philosophy through your athletes; be loyal to your system and follow your chain of command.

You, as a coach, are ultimately responsible for creating that atmosphere of success. I remember Coach Reade speaking with my Augustana College team before our 1986 season, after winning three consecutive national championships. He asked us simply, "Why could it not be us to do it again?" We controlled many of the variables necessary to repeat as champions. So when you are building your program ask yourself, Why not us? Believe that what you are doing will produce the intended outcomes. Your belief system is vital to your own self-confidence as well as to development of a winning culture.

Success may not always come by way of championships, though. Because of that, you may end up doing a lot of the right things but still not keep your job if you are a head coach. That is the inherent risk you take when you pursue that role. Low risk, low reward. I don't prescribe that you focus on your job status, but make sure that if you are going to do something, believe in yourself and do it the right way. Part of that is knowing and following your school, state, and national policies.

There is no shame in losing when you are working hard in an ethical manner. There is shame when you win without integrity. Do the right things. Always keep policies in mind and don't try to get ahead by cutting corners. Ethics is your key and integrity is your lock. They have to fit together.

Have a strong moral compass and make decisions that are in the best interest of your school, program, and athletes. Don't shy away from making the hard decisions, and deal with issues in an ethical manner. Never put relationships or winning ahead of your principles.

A lot of things will change over the course of your career in terms of strategy, schemes, and techniques, but your ethics should not. I can't think of many things more important than your integrity. All the success in the world will not replace it. The foundation you work so hard to build can be destroyed with one bad choice. "What do you benefit if you gain the whole world but lose your own soul?" (Matthew 16:26)

Create a healthful environment for your players, coaches, and athletes. Look out for the wellbeing, health, and safety of your players. Don't compromise safety or put your players at risk under any circumstances. Make sure you make providing protective equipment a priority and work with your training staff in developing safety plans covering a wide variety of potential concerns associated with your sport and activity in general. Be wary of young student drivers and preach good driving habits to them. Don't risk holding a practice if it involves their driving in poor conditions. Be cognizant of your surroundings and environmental conditions such as high temperatures and lightning. Use best practices as related to conditioning, nutrition, and adolescent development.

It is critical for the safety of our athletes and the status of your employment that your athletes are supervised at all times. Even the best of young student-athletes may make poor individual or group decisions from time to time when left on their own. Negligence on the coach's part will have potential career-ending consequences, depending on the severity of the situation. It is just poor practice to risk injuries, harassment issues, and everything in between when we leave our athletes unattended.

Again, you are working with our families' most important possessions, their children, and a bare minimum requirement in our line of work is to provide adequate supervision. Create a safe environment, have control over the situations you manage, and be vigilant to avoid dangerous, risky, or unstructured situations that have the potential to go badly. From the time you arrive on duty to the time the last person leaves, be ever mindful of those responsibilities.

Be respectful of family time and understand that it should be a priority to your coaches, players, and you. Develop a mutual respect for opposing coaches and take the high road when it might be easier to do the opposite. Model sportsmanship and build a positive rapport with officials, believing that they are just like you and do the best they possibly can. You should put your heart and soul into your work and be a tenacious competitor, but in the end you should be able to keep perspective in both winning and losing.

Celebrate success regardless of what that looks like for you. Depending on the progress of your program, a significant accomplishment for you is going to look different from what it might look like in a more established program. Nevertheless, coaches and athletes should feel good about your big moments. Over time, you will continue to elevate the bar, and significant victories will become more substantial. Make sure to commemorate significant career milestones, career firsts, significant wins, and program records when they are achieved. It is a good way to bring attention to the results of hard work and serves to motivate aspiring young athletes.

Build confidence in your players and use positive affirmations to help them believe they are capable of great things. Humans have a natural tendency to be competitive and you can coax that primal nature out of them. I heard a story once of a successful program that incorporated competition in almost every aspect of practice. They believed that it would enhance their performance. There may be something to that philosophy, as the program is one of the most consistently successful ones in the country in their particular sport. Talent is important, but the mental aspect of training and competition can make the biggest difference in success.

Build confidence in your program so that your athletes look forward to big challenges. Great coaches show confidence in their players so they know they can achieve great things. Push them further than they think they can be pushed, and let them know you think they are capable of becoming better than they think. Help them to become tough-minded and overcome the psychological roadblocks that can limit all of us.

Over the years of coaching, if there was one trait I valued above all else in my athletes, it would be toughness. Not only physical toughness, but mental toughness. When a game is on the line, talent and techniques are important, but without toughness it is hard to put those other qualities to good use. We know that getting to the next level of competition is often bigger in our minds than what it actually takes to get there. Wouldn't you love to go back and do it all over again knowing what you know now?

Experience teaches us that some of the obstacles in front of us are not really as big as our brain makes them out to be. For growth to occur, it is beneficial that we get opportunities to compete against individuals and teams that are better than we are "on paper." Once we have figured out that beating a significant opponent does not take a larger-than-life effort, we will gain the confidence necessary to keep setting bigger goals.

As a coach, you have to show some mental toughness yourself. Move on after wins and losses, as your team will have a difficult time moving forward until you do. Prior to events, you may have to be the calming force that brings some balance to your team. That anxiety that all athletes experience can be paralyzing during competition, if you do not know how to channel that energy and refocus. You have been in situations like that before and can model for them how to keep emotions in check so their nervousness and excitement do not hinder performance.

Coach Darol Snyder often used to remind me to get a grip on my emotions during end-of-the-season wrestling tournaments because I had a tendency to wear them on my sleeve, which could create some pre-match tension. Give your athletes the tools they need so they can deal with the distractions and self-doubt that start to creep into their minds when they most need to be focused on the task at hand. All athletes experience these feelings, but the best learn to perform in spite of it.

Work to develop tough-minded attitudes. One of the more unconventional things I tried as a coach was to read our wrestlers segments of a book each night on the mental aspect of training. Over the years of coaching, I became convinced that the mental aspect of most sports, and certainly wrestling, created the greatest obstacles that needed to be overcome in order to succeed.

By reading the book, we were able to talk about situations that all athletes experience and how to best overcome those roadblocks. It had such a significant impact on our performance that every season after that, we found a new book to read.

We often sense when our teams are ready to compete, and much of that has to do with the mindset of our individuals and teams before the game. Developing the right frame of mind can help them ascend to new heights. In 2007 our wrestling team qualified for a program-first trip to the state dual tournament. We were the 7th seed out of 8, so we got matched up against a perennial power and 2nd seed for our opening match. We did not match up well with this traditional powerhouse that was highly favored in our meet.

Because of inclement weather, the meet to take place on Saturday was postponed until the following Monday, and our team was forced to practice over the weekend. Once again our coaching staff got together to see how we might shuffle our lineup to give us a better edge against our opponent.

In the end, we decided to go with the guys who got us there. The athletes were a little irritable because of the extended weekend, and when we started practice, you could tell there was a little different level of intensity in the wrestling room.

During the first 15 minutes of live wrestling practice, a little scuffle broke out between two of our wrestlers. An assistant coach jumped in and made them shake hands and get back to wrestling. Five minutes later, one of our ranked seniors got cut above his eye, and we sent him to the hospital to receive stitches. Ten minutes later, we had another minor injury due to the intensity of practice. At that moment, instead of looking around and wondering how much worse it could get, I realized for the first time that the team we were wrestling the next day was going to be in for quite a battle because of our team mindset.

As it turns out, we wrestled at an entirely different level against that formidable opponent. We did not even have to put on the mat our wrestler who had received stitches the day before, because we had the meet wrapped up at that point. It was a great example of how attitudes can be the driving force to success.

On a side note, besides the win being a historic first for our program, every wrestler who wrestled in that match had gone through our entire program starting with our youth club. That success created a deep sense of pride in our overall program.

Surround yourself with leaders and people of high character. Find coaches who are like-minded in your passion for success. You will not be able to direct every aspect of your program, nor would you want to. There are not enough of you to go around or time in the day to accomplish everything that needs to be done. On top of that, you don't want to micro-manage your staff. Don't think you have to have all the answers. There are some great coaches out there who can help your program ascend to the next level.

One way to build trust and ownership in your program is to delegate responsibility to your coaches. That being said, you want to be confident that in your absence, things are going to be handled the right way. It may not be exactly as you would have done it, but when you have good people on staff you don't have to worry about the fundamental aspects of your program such as ethics and integrity. You will also know your staff is treating young people the way you would want them treated.

Make sure everyone knows that the things you are trying to do are vitally important to your success. You should always work to streamline your program by evaluating every aspect of it regularly and identify the things that are not efficiently meeting your criteria of importance. Nothing is worse than everyone spending a lot of time on things that did not have a particular purpose or were perceived as a waste of time. Whether you run a short practice or a long one, it should be managed efficiently. Your time together is extremely valuable and should be productive and not seem to drag on.

Everyone should see your passion and enthusiasm. You are not a lesser coach by smiling, laughing, or having a good time. You might be surprised to see the positive response you get from your athletes if you break out of your shell and let them see a part of you they would never have guessed even existed. Your business is a people business with real emotions and feelings. You will need to show compassion as well as understanding. Great leaders are also great listeners.

Don't turn your back on your athletes when they struggle or fail, or show excitement and content only when they are winning. That is not what coaching is about. Just as you are going to continue to challenge your athletes when they are having success, continue to coach them through adversity. If you tear them down, you have to build them back up.

Be there for them when they need you the most. Athletes and parents want to know you will be there for them during good times and bad. Be mindful of your body language, as it paints the picture of your attitudes as clearly as your words tell the story.

Make sure your students understand how critical their education is to them. Personal qualities that make them successful in athletics are the same skills they will need to succeed in the classroom and vice versa. Stay on top of their academic progress so that no one is surprised when they are having trouble in a class, and you can help intervene. Provide opportunities for tutoring or study tables if they don't have the self-discipline to correct the problems they are having on their own.

I once surprised a group of athletes by meeting them after practice in my classroom, where I had also invited their parents so that we could discuss their lack of progress in some of their classes, including mine. The parents, of course, appreciated the meeting more than the athletes. I also coached an athlete who was falling behind in an English class he was taking. I worked with the teacher so that I could help get him caught up, and after practice we would return to my office and read poetry a couple of times a week. We were not always in a great frame of mind directly after an intense practice, but as coaches we do what it takes for our athletes to succeed. On other occasions, I would invite athletes to our home in the evenings to help them get caught up on a subject or study for a test. Jenny always seemed to have something special for them to eat and drink.

The message here is that sometimes you have to go well beyond the call of duty to make sure your athletes are successful. You do whatever it takes within ethical and legal boundaries. There is no doubt everyone will have an appreciation for the things you do and you will have a sense of satisfaction when you see them have success in both academics and athletics. As a coach, you have a chance to leave a legacy on your athletes, program, school, and community. That legacy can be long-lasting and should go well beyond your career record.

I recently watched some of the interviews regarding Frank Beamer's retirement from his 29-year career as the head coach of the Virginia Tech football program. Upon losing their final home football game at Lane Stadium in an emotional overtime game, his players hoisted him on their shoulders and carried him off the field. By all reports, Coach Beamer was an exceptional coach and earned personal accolades as he led his program to great success. But in listening to him discuss his long coaching tenure at the university, I heard him mention first and foremost the respect and caring that everyone had for each other, not the success. He was quite grateful for the opportunities the school had given him. He created a family-like atmosphere and a winning culture while he was there.

GAME DAY

The post-season is not mathematically out of the question but we don't control some things that will have to happen. It is disappointing for everyone, considering what looked to be ahead of us. With all our history, tradition, expectations, rankings, and players, the one great thing about any athletic season is that you earn each and every thing you get. Good or bad. There is no sure bet, and games or seasons are not predetermined. We will show some character with three games left and rebound as a team.

What has turned out to be a very special relationship is about to come to an end: four Maass boys spanning seven years on our varsity team. Since 2003 I have had the privilege of coaching Andy '03-'04, Alex '05-'06, Will '06-'07, and Wes '08-'09. There have been many other brothers to go through the program including the three Jones boys — Ryan, Ross, and Riley — but four does not happen often. All four Maass boys have been different, and each had his own unique character.

Andy was a tough offensive guard, a performer who didn't need a lot of attention but quietly got the job done. Alex had a season lost due to ACL injury, but his leadership during that season and his comeback as a senior made him one of the best leaders I have ever coached. Will, an All-State player, was one of those unique athletes who probably could have played any position and done it well. Probably his greatest gift to our program was his unselfishness in playing the offensive line even when he would rather have been at a skilled position. This gift was the catalyst to our first district championship and quarterfinal team. Will was also the one who knew how to "push my buttons" and I think he enjoyed doing it from time to time. The story is not over for Wes, the youngest, but he has been a consistent performer for two years on both sides of the ball and has carried on the Maass tradition.

The strong dynamic with these four has been the role of Klaus and Jennifer Maass, their parents. If you have ever wondered what kind of role you should take when your sons or daughters enter high school athletics, look no further than the example set by these two.

I am certain over the past seven seasons of coaching the Maass boys that I made some poor decisions and maybe did some things that Jennifer and Klaus didn't agree with. But I would never have known it. Their four boys were not always starters or on winning teams. They were not always selected captains or All-District players. Sometimes they may even have gotten the short end of the stick, for example when Will was overlooked by the Shrine Committee. But good or bad, their associations with me have always been positive and I admire them for that.

They have been the type of people to show public support for their kids as well as for our program. I never felt that I wanted to avoid talking with them because of football, how their kids were playing, or how the team was doing. I would always see Klaus, after a long day at work, in his purple and gold working concessions, grilling for the Boosters on Friday nights, or helping in many other volunteer projects in his free time. He might give me a simple "Good Luck!" or "Are the guys ready?" which has always been combined with that great grin and contagious laugh. Jennifer started the hoop girl tradition and game-day locker decorations, and also helped in the organization of parent groups to continue meals, yard signs, rallies, and other items.

Having sons or daughters compete at any age can become nerve-wracking, especially when you have an emotional investment. You want what is best for them — but so does everyone else. I admire Klaus and Jennifer for not becoming bitter, negative people when things didn't end up perfect or go their way. Instead, they did something I would recommend for everyone: Enjoy each and every moment! Life is too short not to take great memories from your children's participation in sports, and the Maass family has many of them to enjoy.

In reality, whether they win or lose, or whether they were stars or role players are such minor issues in the overall significance of participation in a young person's life. Not to give them unconditional support from home, especially when it would be easy to go the other way, is a waste of precious time. I know that none of the four Maass boys were perfect at practice or games, and I am guessing they drove their parents crazy from time to time. But there is a great chance that these four guys will perpetuate the kind of love and support with their own kids because they had great role models.

Most people know that coaches, especially young coaches, get driven out of the profession by parents. If you have ever coached at any level you know what I mean. Most coaches can deal with poor performance by players or disappointing seasons. They have experience with both good and bad seasons themselves and know how to handle it along with all the "issues" presented by young student-athletes who might need a little "guidance" from time to time. But it can be parental scrutiny of a coach's decision-making, questioning of playing time or play calling, and unrealistic expectations that make it tough to coach. Like almost everyone else, coaches generally do the best they can. The difference is that most other professions don't involve someone else's most prized possessions — their kids. Coaches sometimes take personally those negative interactions with a few cynical parents, but the fact is they are a minority.

On the other side of the coin are the many great parents like Klaus and Jennifer whom I have gotten to be around in the past 23 years, who have made me proud to work here on behalf of their kids. I could make a long list of the ones I know, but some quietly supported and enjoyed the experience without my ever knowing who they were at all. Thanks to all of you on that list and a special thanks to Klaus and Jennifer Maass, who made the past seven years so special.

> *"Every morning in Africa, a gazelle wakes up. It knows it must run faster than the fastest lion or it will be killed. Every morning a lion wakes up. It knows it must outrun the slowest gazelle or it will starve to death. It doesn't matter whether you are a lion or a gazelle... when the sun comes up, you'd better be running."*
>
> —Unknown

CHAPTER 5 ACTIVITIES

- Describe the current climate or culture of your program.

- How would you characterize your leadership style?

- Identify a change you would like to make to your athletic culture and how you might achieve that through a modification of your leadership style.

- List 3 ways you can make your season significant to all the members of your team and make them feel valued regardless of their role or talent level.

- In what ways can you help your athletes develop the mental aspects of competition and training?

This 1986 Augustana College, Rock Island, Ill., football team won an unprecedented fourth consecutive national championship. I was a senior on this team (front No. 42). Coach Bob Reade is in the back row, far right. *Photo courtesy of Augustana College Sports Information Department, Rock Island, Ill.*

Youth baseball was one of the first organized teams I played on. I am at top right and my brother, Eugene, is at bottom left. Our coach, in back, was Richard Swanson.

I also got a chance to wrestle at Augustana College. Head Coach Dennis Riccio, also football defensive coordinator, was an influential coach. *Photo courtesy of Augustana College Sports Information Department, Rock Island, Ill.*

Athletics has always been an important part of my life. I enjoyed my time as a competitor at North Scott High School, Eldridge, Iowa, as a Lancer (inset), and I had as much fun over the years as a football and wrestling coach. *Photo courtesy of The Observer, DeWitt, Iowa.*

Coach Darol Snyder and I are certainly wrapped in the emotions of this match with Coach Ed Vance, back, looking on.

Coach Kreiter, center, with the Maass boys — Will, Wes, Andy, and Alex. Three of the Maass brothers wrestled and all of them played football between 2003 and 2010.

Kevin Wulf was an outstanding and hardworking wrestler and football player for the Sabers. He went on to proudly serve our country in our military.

Three Saber greats who went on to play at the college level were Tyler Driscoll (No. 34) and Michael Walter (No. 45) for St. Ambrose University, Davenport, Iowa. Sam Schmidt (No. 44) played for the University of Wisconsin, Platteville. It was always a special moment to celebrate great times with them. *Contributed photos this page.*

Chad Rowson, state wrestling champion, has become a park ranger for the Department of Natural Resources in Iowa. He coaches his three sons through a youth wrestling program in his community of Pleasantville, Iowa.

This 2007 Saber football team became the first team at Central DeWitt to win district titles. The 2008 team became the fifth team in school history to finish the regular season undefeated. This photo was taken after our last regular season win. On far left are Coach Ryan Streets in dark jacket and Coach Shane Sikkema in light jacket. In back row, far right to left, are coaches Tony Foxen, Cody Schultz, Jered Birt, Ed Vance, Kurt Kreiter and Terry Daniels. *Photo courtesy of* The Observer, *DeWitt, Iowa.*

The 2007 Saber wrestling team became the first team in school history to qualify for the state dual meet tournament. They finished fourth place in Class 2A. This group picture was taken in Central DeWitt's wrestling room following our qualifying win to advance to the state dual tournament in Cedar Rapids, Iowa. On the left are coaches Don Salyars with Kurt Kreiter, and on right are Darol Snyder and Mike Murphy, and Ed Vance, front. *Photo courtesy of* The Observer, *DeWitt, Iowa.*

Top: The first team I (top left) got a chance to coach as a head coach in 1987, with assistant coach John Fury (top right), high school friend and teammate.

Middle: The development of youth programs with the help of great volunteers is instrumental to program success. Top row: Kurt Kreiter, Kirk Azinger, Doyle Fox, Brian Klinefelter, Rex King, Don Salyars.

Bottom: The 2006 team shows off their brackets after their sectional wrestling championship title. On far left is Coach Don Salyars, with Coach Rick Steward sixth from the left. From far right, are coaches Kirk Azinger, Kurt Kreiter, Darol Snyder and Ed Vance. *Photos on this page courtesy of* The Observer, *DeWitt, Iowa.*

87

Learn as much as you can from your coaching peers. Here I am working at a JV wrestling meet with two Hall of Fame coaches: Tom Kilburg of Western Dubuque, Iowa, left, and Jeff Tampir of Maquoketa, Iowa, center.

This was a great moment for our school and for me personally. Legendary Coach Dan Gable is one of the greatest athletes and coaches in American sports history. Having him speak at our school for National Library Week was special to me.

We take great pride when our former athletes like state finalist Adam Grell (above) join the coaching ranks. I later got a chance to coach with Adam at Central DeWitt, and here we are shouting instructions to one of our wrestlers (above, left). Behind Coach Grell is Tom Danner, National Hall of Fame wrestling coach, watching the match in progress. Our program is now in the hands of two of our former wrestlers, Head Coach Matt Ohnemus and Assistant Coach Adam Grell, who (left) congratulate Nick Smith after a win. *Photos on this page courtesy of* The Observer, *DeWitt, Iowa.*

Haley and I walk off the track after her last race. I enjoyed watching her, but eventually competition comes to an end.

Casey and I share a proud moment after he snapped in his first NFL game for the Denver Broncos at Mile High Stadium.

Casey and Haley during the state track meet. I loved watching them compete.

I had a great time coaching both with and against my brother, Eugene, left. Casey, center, hopes to coach someday.

It was always fun having Haley keeping our playlist on the sideline.

With Casey and Haley both attending the University of Iowa, Jenny and I became avid Hawkeye supporters and enjoyed our time traveling to games.

Chapter 6

BUILDING A COMMUNITY
Your Program

"At last the ladder,
which had been built slowly, slowly,
one hope at a time, reached up to the clouds.
And the dreamer began to climb."

—Katherine Berry

Being the head coach of two very different programs gave me a great appreciation for the difference between various sports when building a program. Football is a sport that embraces the masses and is well known for its popularity. Wrestling has a real sense of community associated with it, and if you are in that community you are typically quite passionate about it.

Although football has its own challenges, it was considerably easier to recruit athletes and their families into the football program because of the familiarity of the sport. It took considerably more effort to market wrestling to athletes who were unfamiliar with what we had to offer.

There is strength in numbers, so developing and expanding your base of athletes is always a good goal for your programs. The more athletes you have participating, the better the competition is going to be at practice. The better the competition at practice, the better your chance of developing a competitive team. The more competitive your team, the better chance you have to succeed.

Although I don't think I would be good in the business world, coaches really do become salesmen at times. There are many things to consider when building a program within your district and community that will help you create a positive atmosphere in regard to what you are trying to accomplish. The more you expand your coverage and the more you can make others feel they are part of it, the better your chances to build something special.

VISIBILITY

Expanding your coverage by becoming visible in your community will also mean that you will take some risks in making yourself vulnerable when you are available to the public. Many coaches have experienced a few bad encounters with someone wanting to talk about the program in an inappropriate manner or time. If you have not experienced these critics, stick with it and you will. Someone will surely want to discuss some aspect of your program with you when you are out and about in non-school related situations.

Visibility is necessary even if you have to be subjected to a few awkward conversations from time to time. Use discretion in your public discussions about your program. Familiarity breeds contempt. People who feel they know your program well may feel entitled to voice criticism. Some people don't have very good filters or may not understand social etiquette when you are in the community doing something as basic as grocery shopping. You may even have to develop a strategy for handling those situations so that you don't become reclusive in your community or alienate your family, who occasionally may have to endure a few inappropriate interruptions, too.

My wife, Jenny, selected her seat carefully when attending football games. She is a snappy Italian, so she had no problem discussing in a direct manner any questions someone may have had about her husband and coaching. But she did want to avoid some of those uncomfortable confrontations when she and our children, like many others in our community, were trying to enjoy a Friday night football game. Our daughter, Haley, was shocked one year when she was standing in line at a local sandwich shop and heard some disparaging remarks about her dad from two others standing in line in front of her. She could not believe someone would say such things.

Of course, those encounters happen infrequently and are part of our business. At times you have to have blinders on and earplugs in when you are leading a program. Stay focused and believe in what you are doing. One of the most necessary components in helping you build your community is self-confidence. When someone makes a critical remark, it does not qualify as truth. Coaching can be a volatile profession and you have to show some grit at times or you are not going to survive. Don't be afraid to put yourself out there with confidence and show the public what you stand for and who you are. In time you will gain the respect from those supporting you.

Get to know your community and the resources available to you. Let them know that your interests go well beyond the school and competition. Make it a point to seek out and visit your community leaders and offer your services where you can help. You might be asked to speak to the local Rotary Club or Lions Club about your program. Take advantage of all speaking engagements. Many great volunteer organizations promote service activities you and your team leaders could be a part of. Get involved in your community to help shed a positive light on your own program as well.

Learn the history of your program and become responsible for being the historian of your program. Community members will appreciate that fact that you embrace your history and intend to add to the legacy.

I knew a coach who entered a community that had a great program tradition. He made the decision that he would strip the walls of all the historic pictures and records, because he was directing a new era, and they were not going to live in the past. This made for a brief opportunity as head coach in that district, and those pictures are now back up on the walls.

The historic names and accomplishments are a source of great pride for a program, school, and community. Even if you do not have any history with the program, embrace it and be proud of it. You are now part of that history. Make program records visible, as they can serve as a source of inspiration in your program and motivation for young athletes aspiring to do big things.

If you are a head coach and plan on building a comprehensive program, it is critical that you get involved and oversee all the different levels of your program. Your contract may read that you are the head coach at one specific level, but in reality your involvement at all levels is necessary to develop program continuity, which will more easily allow your athletes to transition from one level to another. It will be easier to build your program if it is not fragmented from one level to the next.

That does not mean you have to micro-manage the other levels of your program. All coaches require and deserve a little anonymity and freedom. But they will be looking for and will appreciate your direction and support. It will help your cause if everyone is pulling in the same direction. Create opportunities to share your vision of the program with coaches at your different levels. Communicate your standards and guidelines and help educate coaches as to what you are trying to accomplish. Offer your service and support and be willing to help them out with anything they might need at their particular level. Coaches want to be granted some creative latitude, but helping them implement what you feel is developmentally appropriate at each level will let them know you are actively involved in all aspects of your program.

YOUTH PROGRAMS

It may come full circle again, but the days of kids organizing their own activities with friends and neighbors on a large scale may be a thing of the past. Historically, those situations served as a great way for youth to develop leadership skills on their own, independent of adults. Kids learned for themselves how to organize, officiate, and interact with their peers.

Most of us started dabbling in organized sports during our youth, and some of our best memories from childhood happened when no adults were present. Some of my brother's and my best sports memories were on the farm where we had, in our minds at least, the most classic whiffle ball stadium in the world. With an old barn serving as the Big Red Monster, pasture fence in center, and chicken house in right field, we played countless games on our gravel infield with friends Chuck Ritchie and John Fury. When we could convince more friends to come and join us, we hoped the day would never end. That type of childhood freedom is becoming more and more rare all the time. Today, we tend to organize everything for our children.

There has been much discussion in recent years about how the over-involvement of youth in organized sports can have a potentially negative impact on adolescent development. Sometimes overzealous parents or inappropriate coaching can inflict damage on a youth program or the kids themselves. Sometimes too much or too intense competition too soon in their lives can cause youth to lose interest, or worse yet, create an increased risk of injury.

I am always amazed at how much time, and sometimes money, is invested in our very young by way of organized practice and weekend competitions. Some of the uniforms and equipment they have available are nicer than what some schools with limited budgets have the ability to purchase. At times a significant financial commitment has to be made in order to participate and be part of weekend trips and tournaments. These can be fun experiences, but a lot of thought has to go into making decisions with our youth if we hope to see them continue participation for years to come. We should also be cognizant that some of these experiences can be cost-prohibitive for some families, so provide alternatives so that these events don't become exclusionary.

Despite a few negatives associated with organized youth athletics, these programs create some great family time and fun memories. Many great youth coaches promote enduring qualities that are not exclusive to higher levels of competition. What is important is that wise perspective is developed during those early years. Some parents with ulterior motives may believe that their investment in providing those opportunities will equate to future success. Unfortunately, that is not necessarily the case. Be mindful of the overzealous parent or the one who uses the word "we" when referring to a son's or daughter's participation.

I have heard various opinions and have seen formulas as to how much competition is age-appropriate and when and how a young person should start involvement in organized athletics. I don't know if there is one definitive answer that covers all sports and all situations, but I do know there is not a better time in history for good veteran coaches to get involved in youth sports and serve as a voice of reason and bring some perspective to sports based on their own experiences and expertise.

I am a strong believer that your program involvement should also extend to youth levels. Organize local camps and clinics that are affordable for all your youth. Better yet, try to run them for free to allow your athletes to grow as athletes without having to travel great distances or pay large sums of money for instruction. Youth programs are a great way to get parents introduced to your program and philosophy. We coaches know the real benefits of young people participating and the positive influence youth programs can have on a young person. Involve your entire staff to help you run those events. They are great opportunities to engage your community.

Talk to your elementary, intermediate, or middle school physical education teachers and encourage them to run introductory units for your sport. If they do, make sure to provide them all the support and resources they will need to make it a quality unit.

Encourage your older athletes to get involved at the younger levels of your program. They can serve as great mentors and ambassadors of your sport. It will be a great opportunity for them to use their leadership skills and to make an impact on youth. Upperclassmen sometimes fail to remember that our young participants are no different from what they were at that age. They knew who was competing at the high school level and held them in high regard. Most of us had older athletes in our school who served as role models. I know I did.

Organize bus trips to local college games for your youth and players. Some of your kids may never have had the opportunity to watch an event at that level, so attending a game or meet will be a great time and can be eye-opening to your youth. Invite youth teams to sit behind your bench at a contest, or take a real leap of faith and invite a youth team into the locker room at halftime to experience what that is like. Use good discretion and judgment or the intended results might backfire on you. Celebrate your youth organizations with a Youth Night where you honor all your players, coaches, and volunteers. You might even have them scrimmage during an intermission. Above all else, make sure they know that their participation is important to you.

I had the opportunity to be involved in the ground-floor development of our DeWitt Youth Football program. Great youth volunteers with a like-minded vision for our program were critical to our success. Geoff Blandin, Terry Daniels, Kurt Daniels, Doug Hinkle and many others have helped create a quality organization for our youth.

This local organization provides organized tackle football opportunities for our fifth- and sixth-graders. At the onset it also provided opportunities for our seventh-graders before that level was absorbed into our middle school program. We were organized locally and played games in a league at a bigger city 20 minutes to our east.

Our youth football board thought it was important for us to divide our teams equally so that each of our teams received an equitable amount of skill, speed, and size. This division likely lessened our chance of winning the league title, but we felt that the benefits would serve our program much better for future success. Our community has since added a flag football league, which was established for our first-through sixth-grade youth. Over the years, I also took the time to organize a local competition of the National Football League's Punt, Pass, and Kick event, as an additional way to promote the sport and give back to youth.

Prior to my arrival at Central DeWitt, the former Mat Rats wrestlers had disbanded. Knowing the importance of a youth wrestling organization to our overall program, I took over a parks and recreation program run by our city to develop our youth wrestling organization, the Sabertooth Wrestling Club, from its inception. Working with great youth volunteers like Pat Clark, Doyle and Lisa Fox, Rex King, Don Salyars, Brian Klinefelter, Kirk Azinger and many others over the years made my job as a coach much easier and provided our youth a fun opportunity to learn and appreciate the sport of wrestling.

When you take on a project like this you may want to come up with a catchy, creative, and positive name. "Sabertooth" worked nicely since our school mascot is a Saber, so the name portrayed some connection to our school program.

Developing a great logo with some catchy letterhead can also help generate a positive image in your community. Have a local artist draw something that you will market on everything you produce. We used that marketing at youth camps, youth tournaments, Fourth of July floats, swim parties, whiffle ball games, on T-shirts, and other events. Over time, the word got out that we had a fun organization for our youth. We also made sure to make it the cheapest club in town and charged just enough to cover the cost of their AAU status and a T-shirt. For those who struggled to meet those costs or for those who had to pay a large sum because of large families, we absorbed the cost ourselves or leaned on private donations. We made sure that we could give the same opportunities to all of our young people.

It is important to get involved in your youth organizations, which introduce sports to our youth. That exposure can make a positive influence on them at a young age. As they say, "You have only one chance to make a first impression," so having the right philosophy in place and the right people sending the right messages is critical to that success. Work closely with the leadership of these groups to make sure your youth will have a productive and fun experience. It is your responsibility to get involved, and it is the group's responsibility to either work with you or get out of the way while you are building your program. Your relationship should not be adversarial. Work alongside and support your youth organizations and local Park & Recreation leaders, as they certainly will help make an impact on what you are doing as well.

Youth programs run the right way can bolster your numbers and help develop a critical foundation for later success. You always want to make sure you don't lose sight of the fact that these experiences are intended to be fun. We had a successful high school wrestler who said the sole reason he kept coming back to participate in our youth wrestling club was that the club played dodge ball at the end of practice! You will have many youth who will not continue to participate as the years pass, but they can still be introduced to the positive aspects of your sport through their involvement and gain a lifelong appreciation for your sport.

Learning how to deal with the emotional highs and lows of competition is part of the maturation process for our youth and their parents. Don't let the scoreboard or records become your measuring stick of contentment and satisfaction. Find ways to get everyone involved. It is difficult to nurture growth unless everyone has a chance to participate. Young athletes will develop a greater sense of value when someone gives them a chance.

Continue to invest your time in all your youth. You never know when young people are going to develop physically or how they might improve over time. As they mature, they may discover other qualities to help them succeed such as hard work, skill development, and self-discipline, to name just a few. As they build the necessary characteristics to match their physical maturity, they will likewise become better competitors. Most likely, you are not going to know the results of that process until they have fully matured.

Even if they stop their participation before they get to that point, their experience should still be a rewarding one in their lives. We have all seen athletes who excelled as youth but tapered off or lost interest as they got older. We have also seen many young people do just the opposite. We are never fully aware how that process is going to play out. It is not realistic or fair to pigeonhole young persons into a certain position or dismiss their abilities because they are not good at a certain developmental age.

Today, those who do not make the cut for the local traveling team may be relegated to Park & Recreation leagues. Thank goodness those

Park & Recreation leagues still exist, because it is a real shame to give up on such a young person, regardless of talent. I think of what a positive impact sports made on my life at a young age and what a disservice it would be to all youth not to give them those same experiences.

Like many other fathers, I volunteered to coach Little League baseball. It was a Park & Recreation league, which at the time was about all that was offered. One of the great youth coaches in our community, Brian Klinefelter, coached the team with me. He also coached our youth wrestling program for many years and shared similar values and philosophy regarding youth sports. We both felt that it was important for every kid to play every position and sit out the same amount of time.

Because of that, some parents declined to enroll their own children on our team, feeling they were too talented to have to take their turn occasionally and sit out a few innings to make room for a less talented child. I can't recall what our record was during those years, but who really does? Don't get me wrong, I love competition and winning, but in the end, does it really matter what your Little League record was? It's not about success or failure, it is about development and the experience.

A great example of this maturation process occurred in our own household. As a freshman in high school, our son, Casey, was not a defensive starter. Like most young people, he came home one afternoon discouraged after practice because he had set goals for himself that were not being met on his timeline. He complained and we listened. He reviewed all the things he had done in the off-season to justify his complaint. He lifted weights, attended speed and agility workouts and off-season skills, drills, 7-on-7, camps, and other activities. For his age, he was self-engaged as a developing player.

In my position as a head coach, it would have been easy for me to pull his coaches aside and plead his case. Instead, our advice at home was to encourage him to keep on doing what he was doing. An athlete does all of those things, and more, not to secure a spot on the field but instead to prepare for competition. When the time is right, that athlete will be better prepared to compete. No one can predict when that time will come, but it is important to be ready. All a player can do is control his or her own attitudes and efforts.

A few weeks later, the teammate who was playing in front of Casey was injured in a game and Casey got his opportunity. He played great in replacement and left such an impression on his coaches that they found a way to keep him on the field the rest of the year. The foundation he was building for himself only improved as he got older. As he became more physically developed, his body merged with his attitudes and work ethic.

Casey went on to become an All-Conference and All-State player. As a college walk-on at the University of Iowa, he had to go through that development process all over again to prove himself. My guess is that his past experience gave him a clearer idea of what was needed to achieve his goals. He ended up earning a scholarship, was named a permanent captain, and collected All-Big Ten honors.

Being signed to a free-agent contract by the Dallas Cowboys and eventually becoming a starter for the Denver Broncos may have seemed like an impossible dream when he was a freshman reserve player, but you never know where hard work and a great attitude will take you.

Coaches at every level have been instrumental to Casey's maturation process and he has experienced great mentors throughout his time in sports. One of his greatest influences during those years was one of his youth coaches, Larry Curtis, who had a gift to inspire and motivate our youth. It is important to put into place key individuals like Coach Curtis who will provide positive experiences.

Even though you will have good advice for your parents on having perspective in sports, be prepared to have strong feelings yourself when it is your own children. Be able to give them good advice without being affected by the emotional aspect of sports. This will be challenging, because we all want our children to achieve and it hurts when they struggle.

It is important to look out for their long-term success. How would our son have felt, or what would he have learned, if I had intervened in the process and he later found out he had not earned his success 100 percent by himself? Those lessons are much more important than any success we might have.

Our daughter, Haley, shares the same value system, work ethic, and great attitude. She was an aspiring gymnast in high school, participated in cross-country, and was a good track athlete. But her passion for sports was not the same as her brother's. Her passion was academically based on her professional aspirations. The same qualities she developed and the lessons she learned through her athletic experience, however, benefited her by helping her learn to work toward goals, manage her time, and handle adversity as a speech pathologist. Hard work and great attitudes are qualities we should continue to nurture in our athletes, who will benefit from them in many areas of their life for years to come.

There is a successful high school football program in Iowa that at one time sent a football to the families of all newborns who were announced in their local paper. It was their way of welcoming all new members of their community as part of their ongoing tradition. It's a great concept.

Develop similar ways to make people feel they are a part of your tradition. Create a sense of pride in your program by expanding your exposure throughout your schools and community. Youth organizations are important, and understanding how they fit into the overall athletic programs must be taken into account.

PARENTS

Like many schools, we use the night of high school orientation to familiarize the parents of our freshmen with athletic activities available to their son or daughter. I still encourage our individual program coaches to communicate with freshman parents through meetings or documents prior to their season, but this is a good opportunity to have a captive audience. Our handouts contain excerpts from our parent-athlete handbook, including information about the responsibilities of coaches and the responsibilities of parents and athletes. Included is literature about eligibility, the recruiting process, choosing a college, and eligibility at various post-secondary institutions.

I provide them with articles targeting parent involvement in their child's athletic experience. I let them know from time to time as a parent they will develop strong feelings that will be hard to control. I help them understand it is in their best interest to take great care when discussing or acting on these feeling, because it will make an impact on their son's or daughter's participation and the feelings they develop about their own self-worth. There are times when parents need to communicate with coaches or administration, but at times those conversations go beyond what is warranted. Similarly, parents need to be careful about what they discuss at home about their child's teams, teammates, and coaches, because their children will most often adopt their parents' opinions and attitudes.

At the same time I am talking with our parents, I dismiss our freshman athletes to the gymnasium where a group of senior athlete leaders have a breakout session as a player panel, moderated by a few of our coaches. It provides opportunity for new athletes, in the absence of their parents, to ask questions as to what life as a high school athlete is like. Our seniors, likewise, can hearken back to the day when they were timid, nervous freshmen and use their experiences to ease some of their fears. Both meetings are great to promote our programs and build a community of trust.

High school sports has the potential to be rewarding in a young person's life, but this will not occur if athletes develop cynical attitudes associated with resentment, poor self-worth, and feelings that they somehow have been cheated out of opportunities. Parents are playing with fire if during their child's participation they nurture a link between their self-worth and the value they place on themselves with winning and losing in sports. When the competition comes to an end, parents may have created self-esteem issues or a rift in their own parent-child relationship.

What purpose is served if we win all the championships in the world and our children do not develop the attitudes and personal qualities that will allow them to achieve when they face bigger challenges in life? Achievement through sports is not the measure of the quality of a person's life.

When it comes to parental involvement at practice, coaches must make certain they think through the decision to have open or closed practices. Your decision should be in line with your standards, philosophy, and school policies. It is not a question of hiding something secretive in a practice or feeling intimidated by parents' presence, because there should never be anything occurring in a practice you need to hide from a parent. Allowing parents to attend practices, however, has the potential to place additional pressure on their children.

It will be hard for some parents to make that transition if they have been heavily involved with their children through youth athletics. Separation may be the best thing to move forward at certain developmental stages. What some parents may perceive as trying to help may in reality create roadblocks to development. It is often fun to showcase what you are doing, but you will quickly learn the warning signs regarding "helicopter" parents.

A few times I have had to stand firm on my values and philosophy when interacting with parents. This was intimidating at first, but in the end it served to strengthen my resolve as a coach. On a few occasions the parents, just like athletes, came back later and thanked me for providing some perspective in their life at a time when they had lost it. There were also a few times when those interactions created a greater divide.

Refusing to compromise on the things you truly believe, however, will make you a better and more confident coach in the end. You do not want to become a coach who will give up your principles to appease a parent or a situation you do not believe in.

Get to know your parents and don't be afraid to have honest discussions with them. Most of them appreciate your honesty and perspectives, even though there will be times when it seems they are fighting you every step of the way. The vast majority of your interactions will be positive ones; like you, parents want what is best for their son or daughter.

Although it can be enjoyable to talk to parents who are attending the games, they can become so engaged in their child's participation that they are not quite as relaxed as they should be. You may have to remind parents from time to time to remember one important fact: enjoy each and every moment, because when it is gone, it is gone for good. You will never get those special times back.

Grandparents, on the other hand, likely will be supporting their grandchild for pure enjoyment and pride. They have already experienced the daily highs and lows of raising teenagers. They have seen the long-term positive impact when young people are involved in extracurricular activities and don't get as wrapped up in wins, losses, and playing time. They take a simpler approach when attending events: They are there to enjoy watching the event and take great pride in watching their grandchildren doing something worthwhile. They fully understand that these are great times in a young person's life to be enjoyed and celebrated. Grandparents who take that approach can be nurturing.

When I can, I share articles with our parents that can bring a perspective to how they may feel as they watch their children experience both success and failure. More important, these articles give parents insight as to how their interactions make their adolescents feel. You may have to help some parents understand that their feelings, expressed through words and actions, can produce the opposite effect of what they intended. Sometimes, what parents say and do is not always viewed in the same way by their child. What was intended as encouragement may be viewed as criticism. Even supporting young athletes through the use of suggestions could be interpreted as disappointment that the athlete has not lived up to certain expectations. If we want our athletes to be supported unconditionally while they participate, they must feel that from the ones they love.

An athlete's memory doesn't often include a detailed recollection of wins and losses; instead, the experiences and relationships with teammates are the things that last. Parents can hold sacred all of the great memories of watching their kids participate but will miss things as simple as talking about practice at the dinner table when it's all over.

We can only hope that all of the tense feelings, frustrations, and concerns that go along with watching our kids participate don't get in the way of experiencing something special.

Challenge all of your young people to go out and make some great memories with their teammates, coaches, parents, grandparents, and most important — themselves!

GAME DAY

I was walking off the practice field last week and in the corner of the game field were two young kids, probably about fourth grade, playing a game of football. It was just the two of them in the corner of the field. I didn't take the dictatorial approach and ask them what they were doing or say, "Hey, you guys need to leave." No, I smiled and imagined that these youngsters had been at the game against Anamosa and while watching our guys were inspired and excited to be on a real game field emulating their favorite players.

I remember playing a full game of football with my brother in our backyard as we were growing up. It was just the two of us in the corner of the field. We were a one-man team. On offense we snapped to ourselves, dropped back to scan the field as if to look for an open receiver or what coverage the only other player was playing, and then threw the ball to the open receiver who was also ourselves. Maybe the reason I like to run the ball offensively is that passing in our one-on-one game was pretty tough. We learned to run tough inside. Occasionally, we got lucky when my dad was not in the field harvesting crops and we could convince him to be the all-time quarterback. Then we felt that we were really big-time.

I would play as my favorite player, John Loussart, from North Scott School District in Eldridge, Iowa. He was a tough farm kid who still holds the single-game tackle record. At a young age there was nothing I wanted to do more than wear the scarlet and gray and be a linebacker like him.

Maybe these two young fourth graders above had watched our game and had argued about who got to be Patrick Gerdes, or they had watched Dylan Azinger and Michael Hedrick come up to make some hard hits and wanted to be them instead. Does this sound crazy? Maybe to Patrick, Dylan or Michael it would, but I would guess they also had their favorite Saber when they were growing up. Now that they are the players, they serve as role models for these young ones who want to grow up to be like them.

We don't always seek to be in leadership or role model positions, but sometimes it is inevitable. We talk to our athletes from time to time about this, and it is the reason that there has to be a higher standard. These athletes are not any better or worse than anyone else, but because they put on a Saber uniform they are held to a different expectation. People are watching. When things go well, we hear about "your football player." When things don't go well, we hear about "your football player." Because these athletes are on the team, situations at school or in the community link them to our team. That is a fact, and our athletes are asked to be aware that their actions are a reflection of our team and football program.

106

Although there is potential for some negatives, I also feel confident our athletes will provide solid leadership and modeling in a positive way for the young hopefuls like the fourth-graders playing football last week on the field. Another generation of inspired Sabers is born.

> *"Start by doing what's necessary;*
> *then do what's possible;*
> *and suddenly you are doing the impossible."*
>
> —St. Francis of Assisi

CHAPTER 6 ACTIVITIES

- Identify 3 assets in your community that would be beneficial to you in building a program.

- Characterize 3 items that drive success in your community, school, and programs.

- Create a couple of goals for each level of your program to fit into your program philosophy.

- List 3-5 fundamental aspects of your program that should be covered at each developmental stage so you have a smooth transition from one level to the next.

- Describe any apprehensions you might have regarding interactions with parents and where you might learn strategies for managing them

Chapter 7

MAKING AN IMPACT
Do the Work

"Yesterday is history. Tomorrow is a mystery.
Today is a gift."

—*Eleanor Roosevelt*

When you put your heart and soul into coaching, you will be motivated to keep looking for ways to enhance your program. Everything you do will take some advance planning and more time than you probably anticipated it would take. Don't feel that you have to do everything you would like to do in building your program during your first season. Truly, I would not recommend it. You will have plenty of activities to tend to that are higher in priority when you are first getting acclimated to being a coach.

Identify a few things you would like to try each year and organize something worthwhile to enhance your program. Whether it is finding new ways to encourage participation, implementing new schemes and strategies, or developing new training regimens, there is always something to do. Quality is more important than quantity. If your new concepts work out as intended you may consider keeping them. If not, you can scrap or revise them. Over the years you will notice that you are doing a great deal more than   you did when you first started, but it will not seem as overwhelming. In any profession, we often become more efficient as we grow. Don't forget to delegate responsibilities or tasks to other staff members if you have that luxury.

BUILD RELATIONSHIPS

It is important that you work with other programs in trying to achieve your program goals. It is easy to get tunnel vision and forget that other coaches are trying to achieve the same things you are and that you may be sharing the same group of athletes. You should be cognizant and respectful of other programs. Be especially aware of what is going on with the in-season sport. Their activities should always take priority. You should be helpful in making sure the athletes you share are not put in situations where they have to make impossible choices.

More and more, our kids are pulled in all sorts of directions as they try to meet the demands of all their programs. Coaching has changed a great deal over the last few decades, especially in the off-season demands that coaches now feel compelled to orchestrate and our communities expect. If your athletes are multiple-sport participants, they may be encouraged to participate in year-round activities for multiple sports.

Time management is critical. Sometimes there is not enough time in the day to do it all, on top of core activities such as strength and conditioning or speed and agility training, as well as their academics, obligations, and the time we all need just to be ourselves.

I strongly believe that having our athletes compete in different activities is still the best way to produce competitors. Be a leader in your collaboration with coaches of other programs and help your athletes deal with the organization of their time. We all know school districts that have high participation in all their programs and complement that with a high level of success across all their sports teams. Those are the programs your school should try to emulate.

What makes it so attractive for athletes to want to participate in all their programs? What allows them to be consistently good in multiple sports? Explore the answers to those questions and I bet you will find a school where coaches are working together.

At one time there was a trend to promote sports specialization. That trend seems to be going in the opposite direction. There are well-documented studies now that detail the negative impact specialization may have on our athletes from a physical, psychological, and motivational standpoint. There are also many well-noted reasons why being involved in a variety of activities benefits the overall wellbeing of our athletes. Some of the most successful, competitive, and highly recruited college athletes participated in multiple sports during high school. The reality of this concept might look much different if you coach in a large metropolitan school, compared with a smaller rural school.

This emphasis on participation also involves encouraging our youth to explore interests outside the realm of sports. Producing well-rounded students should be a goal of education. There is so much to experience through the fine arts, clubs, and various other organizations both curricular and extracurricular, that it would be a disservice not to promote these activities with our student-athletes. One of the great things about being young is the opportunity we have to learn about our strengths and weaknesses while being involved. Help foster a desire in our youth to be participants in life!

Building a respected program will more easily be achieved when you work in a school where everyone is supportive and rooting for one another. Lead by example and show genuine support for other teams, even if they are in direct competition for your athletes during your season. Others will notice and respect that quality in you. Support the athletes of different sports, wish their coaches well, and attend their games. When you pay attention to what they are doing, you may also notice qualities in their program that you may want to incorporate into your own.

At one time George Pickup, now our high school principal, was a highly successful head basketball coach at the same time I was our head wrestling coach. We were respectful of each other's program and each winter we chose a day to swap our teams during the conditioning

111

period of practice. He would take our wrestlers and put them through his basketball conditioning, and I would do the same for his basketball players in the wrestling room. Wrestling is well known for its tireless workouts, so Coach Pickup's players were always a bit hesitant.

The fact that athletes are in good physical condition doesn't mean they are conditioned for sports-specific activities. So it was good for both groups, and we made it a positive experience. We wanted our programs to share a mutual respect and our athletes to support each other, even though they competed in rival sports during the same season. We felt this was a great way to accomplish both in a creative way. It definitely helped build a positive relationship between our athletes and coaching staffs.

I was raised on a small family farm that was just big enough to provide a livelihood for a family of five, and a great lifestyle for all of us growing up, but my father fell on some tough times during the farm crisis of the 1980s, just about the time my sister, brother, and I were about to head off to college. My mom, who had worked alongside my dad on the farm, was forced to enter the workforce and became a high school secretary. Later, my dad supplemented his income as a substitute night custodian, also at the high school.

Besides the great respect I have for my parents for the sacrifices they made to put all of us through college, I developed the same respect for secretaries and custodians at our school. When administrators are out of the building from time to time during the day, normal business goes on without a hitch. But if a secretary or a custodian were to go missing for any length of time, the school would struggle to operate effectively. They are the backbone of our schools. Coaches should go to great lengths to build a positive relationship with all of their support staff. Secretaries are at the top of that list. Stay in good standing with your custodial and maintenance crew, as well.

Take special care of your team managers because they are some of the most valuable members of your team. Build a rapport with your spirit group leaders; there are many ways to get them involved in your program. If your district is lucky enough to have a trainer, realize how fortunate you are. Even after taking athletic training courses for certification, some coaches don't feel comfortable taping, evaluating, or setting up a rehab regimen. Your trainers are of vital importance to keep your athletes in competition so build a solid relationship with them.

Your cooks, transportation director, and bus drivers will be important to you during a season, so treat them well, too. It requires everyone to make your events run smoothly, so don't take your event workers for granted. This includes statisticians, press box and score table personnel, ticket-takers, volunteers, announcers, event security, team doctors, orthopedists, physical therapists, paramedics, concession workers, boosters, and others. There are lots of people who are vital to your program running smoothly, and they are all important. It is amazing how far a free T-shirt or a meal ticket at an event will go to keep you in their good graces.

PROMOTE YOUR PROGRAM

There will be opportunities for you to promote your program and let people know about all the great things that are happening. Assisting you will be your local and regional newspapers, radio stations, and television stations. Create a media contact list with phone numbers, emails, and fax numbers and help their reporters when you can by keeping them informed about what is going on in your program.

When you coach a more popular sport, reporters may regularly seek you out. If you are coaching a less popular sport, you may have to do some of the legwork yourself to promote your team. Either way, do what is necessary to give your athletes and your teams the best possible exposure. Assign a coach or manager to update social media and to fax or email results after your events. People in the community will want to know what happened if they were not in attendance.

In our area, a local radio personality, Gary Determan of 1340 KROS in Clinton, Iowa, has been doing a Wednesday night sport show with local coaches for more than 40 years. Not only does he interview local coaches about their programs once a week, but he feeds them as well. For me, this radio show was a chance after practice to share stories with other local coaches and pick their brains about their programs. Although it involved another personal sacrifice to miss dinner with my family once a week during the season, it was an important way to promote our program.

Develop pre-season and state-level event previews for the media to use while covering your program. Following this page is an example of a media guide that we shared with our contacts for pre-season and post-season events. Since so many media outlets send out pre-season questionnaires, having a standard form to share with all of them can save you a little bit of time in preparation for your season. This form can be easily modified to create post-season media guides to share with those covering post-season events and your state tournaments. You can also add personal information and addresses or have this form available for college recruiters who send prospect letters or visit your school. I know they appreciate having the additional information available.

I have found that the men and women of the media are really quality people, and I have become friends with some of them over the years. We always made sure to invite our local newspaper sports reporter, Steve Thiltgen, to stay at the same location as our team at the state wrestling tournament. It was great getting to know him on a personal level and socializing between sessions. We also made sure to invite him to our post-event socials we held for workers, coaches, and supporters. It is always fun spending time with sports-minded friends.

Find the tech-savvy person in your program and have him or her design a team website that is attractive, easy to navigate, and full of great information. Our football program began in 1916 and has some fantastic history over all those years. The previous head coaches were as successful as the teams they coached, but none of them were interested in keeping updated records of games and seasons. When I became head coach, I made it a priority to collect and publish that entire history. After 10 years of research, and with the help of our local newspaper, *The Observer*, I collected the names, statistics, and records from archived articles.

In the end, I had something special I wanted to share with our public. I have used the Internet and Web design to showcase our proud history. My displayed history on a blog site includes single game, season, and career records for individuals and teams spanning all that time. It contains series and year-by-year records. It also displays a record of individual All-Conference, All-State and collegiate players, as well as various pictures and highlight clips.

It was quite an undertaking, but it was a great way to learn about our history, gain more insight about our community, and generate pride in our program.

We marked our 100th year of football in 2015, and after reading about all our past players and looking at all the past data, I have put together what I would consider my All-Century team. I would love to share my opinions, but I hesitate, as I anticipate it could create a storm of controversy. Nonetheless, something like historical reference can be a great way to spark interest in your program.

Use Facebook, Twitter, Instagram, and other social media platforms to market your program. They are a great way to connect with those both near and far and keep them informed. If you have Web-streaming capabilities, consider having someone stream events to relatives of your athletes who live too far away to watch in person.

Invite your media contacts via email to special events. Bring attention to your individual and team success with a public sendoff for state-bound athletes and teams. Publicize national signing days for your college scholarship athletes. We recognize our college-bound athletes with a Saber Signing Day to highlight all of our athletes moving on to the college level, regardless of whether they earned a scholarship or not. We organize a brief ceremony and mock signing for all our male and female athletes committed to participating at all college levels. We invite family, current and future coaches, teammates, and media to attend. It allows us to showcase our great talent and model for our young athletes the opportunities they have in front of them.

There are many ways to promote your program if you are just willing to look for them and use a little of your own creativity. Look at other respected programs for new ways to expand what you currently do. Organize a summer golf outing or something similar in which you reach out to your alumni. These promotional events can be a lot of fun and an opportunity to keep the former players in your program engaged. Events like these will take a little legwork to organize but will be well worth your efforts. We used ours as a fundraiser to help finance our off-season wrestling program and participation at the National Freestyle and Greco tournament in Fargo, North Dakota.

2011 Central DeWitt Football Media Guide
http://blog.central-clinton.k12.ia.us/~kkreiter/Site/Welcome.html

Head Coach: Kurt Kreiter (11th Year / 25th at School)   School Address
Assistant Coaches:
Activities Director:
MS Coaches: Phone:
                                                                               Home:
                                                                               Cell:
2011 Record: Fax:
Colors / Mascot: e-mail:
Post Season Appearances: District / Class:
Undefeated Seasons: Conference:

Returning Letterman/Starter*   Grade Position Height Weight GPA Bench 40 VJ Comments/Honors/Work Ethic/Character/Etc.   Other Sports

Others to Watch:

Team Outlook:

Strengths-

Weakness-

District Outlook:

2011 All-State Players
2011 All Eastern Iowa Team
2011 All District 1st Team/2nd Team

Central Football Players Currently Competing at Collegiate Level:

2011 Academic All-State
2011 Academic All-District
2012 Captains
2012 Preseason All-State
2012 Shrine Bowl

Information:
Records:
• JV
• Sophomores
• Freshman

Team posters are another way to create some enthusiasm for your upcoming season throughout your school and community. They can be simple in design or much more elaborately done. Some of our posters were creative and perfectly fit the personality of our team. Our local photographer, Bill Luse, was always helpful in putting the finished

117

product together. We blanketed our school and community, putting up our posters at as many places as we could. They were often displayed at our seniors' graduation parties. Besides being a promotional tool, they ended up as great keepsakes.

While attending a football clinic years ago, I heard a coach describe a publication he created each week of the season to promote the upcoming football game. When I became head coach, I decided it would be a great way for us to publicize what we were doing, too. Each week of our games, I created a multi-page document I titled Game Day. The document highlighted our upcoming game with records, rosters, and starters. It gave a preview of our opponent's team, including some things they might execute. There were historical items, interviews, information regarding our program, and my own thoughts. I have included some of these Game Day writings at the end of each Chapter in this book.

On Friday morning of our games, I would have Game Day available in our lobby, cafeteria, and teacher's lounge for our students and faculty to read. Our business secretary would also post it online so it could be accessed outside our district. I eventually found out that some of our opponents would log in and read it, too, after a longtime rival and good friend, Tony Perkins of Marion, Iowa, contacted me to tell me he enjoyed what I had written. Today, as an athletic director, I have expanded that publication to include all of our school activities and make it available online and through email for people to read after each of our sports seasons.

Banquets are also a great way to showcase your team and promote your program. You can make it a dessert banquet or a potluck, or have no food at all. Include end-of-the-season awards and highlight videos, and use the opportunity to talk about each of your athletes on the team. Include all levels of your program and invite all of your coaches to talk about their particular level or players. You might consider letting your seniors speak about the impact your program has made on them.

Include a summary of your season and some ideas for your underclassmen to consider while training in the off-season. Some seasons are easier to talk about than others, but as I have mentioned already, regardless of records you can always find positive things to talk about, because our athletes give so much effort even when things don't go their way. Don't dismiss an opportunity because of your record. Expand your invitation to include parents, administration, youth leaders, and community members.

Create a nice-looking record book to distribute to your players or give them an electronic version. Include records, statistics, articles, pictures, and anything else you find significant from your season. You can also have each position coach write something about each individual player to include with individual information and statistics. For your seniors, this is a nice way to summarize what they have meant to your program and an opportunity to provide your underclassmen with some valuable information regarding future expectations.

Parents will appreciate your efforts in creating memorabilia that they will be able to look at years later. You will often see these record books proudly displayed at graduation parties. Each year you will keep finding new items to include and this document can end up becoming quite extensive. All of the things you do will take a little work but they will help enhance your program.

Serve as a meeting point to sponsor a collegiate event at your school. We once hosted a wrestling meet between the Division III programs of Augustanta College, Rock Island, Illinois, and Loras College, Dubuque, Iowa. I had been a college wrestler for the Augustana Vikings, so I had a connection with that program. Hall of Fame Coach Randy Steward, a former Central DeWitt graduate, was the head coach of the Loras DuHawks. So we used that connection to expand the coverage of the sport in our community by hosting this meet. Although it took a little effort to pull off the logistics, it was well worth it.

One of my former football coordinators, Ryan Streets, is now a successful head coach at a neighboring school in Anamosa, Iowa. He has done a great job turning around the program and recently did something I had never heard about but absolutely respect. Still living in their community is a former longtime head football coach and friend of mine, Bob Algoe. Coach Streets honored Coach Algoe's contributions to the program at a home game, but he also did something special that night. During the preceding week, Coach Streets had brought Coach Algoe to practice and had him introduce his old offensive schemes to the players. At the game when Coach Algoe was honored, the first offensive series Coach Streets' team ran was a tribute to Coach Algoe's offensive plays from years gone by. It was quite an honor for Coach Algoe, and the athletes loved the unique highlight.

The concept is similar to all the changing uniforms and helmets we see in college football today or throwback uniforms used in other sports. Coach Streets' idea, though, did not cost a dime and will have a long-lasting impact. That type of novel idea is one reason Coach Streets, besides being an exceptional coach, has been able to make such an impact in his community.

There are many things you can do to promote your athletes. It is amazing how taking a little time out of your day to make up a certificate can make such a big difference in your athlete's confidence. Hand out Athlete of the Meet certificates at the beginning of practice in recognition of significant accomplishments at your events. It serves a dual purpose by allowing you to point out some of the qualities you are looking for in front of your team, as well as making some of your athletes feel pretty good in front of their peers.

Any of these efforts can be of great value in promoting your players, and there are many other forms of recognition that can be used to recognize your athletes. One of the most anticipated days of the week at football practice occurred at the end of each Tuesday practice. Just after talking to the team and before sending them home for the day, we asked one of our players to highlight another player. They would speak about the qualities of the person they chose which made them a special part of the team as a teammate. It was not a lengthy speech but the following week, the highlighted player would pick the teammate of his choice to highlight, and so it went on all season. It was a simple yet special moment and it helped build unity in our group. Those highlights were always sincere and powerful.

You might take advantage of theme nights to help you generate community involvement while honoring deserving groups. Organize an

American Hero Night and let your veterans attend your event for free while making a special announcement in honor of their service. You could also initiate a Cancer Survivor Night. Have your players escort a cancer survivor to midcourt between games for special recognition to enhance your Pink-Out or whatever other cause you might be bringing attention to. There is also Staff Appreciation Night or Past-Present-Future Night.

You should have a Youth Night and recognize all the youth, coaches, and volunteers who invest a great time of time and energy into your developmental levels. You could initiate a Legends Night where you bring back and honor standout individuals or teams from your proud history. This could enhance a Hall of Fame induction or event where you retire a historic number.

Of course, you will want to make Senior Night special. Even though we experience many of these over the years as a coach, there is just one for our seniors and their parents. It will be a night they will remember for a long time to come. All of these events will take some planning — Coaching can be a lot of work! — but they will be well worth your efforts to make your players' experience in their short time in your program more significant.

For every sport, you may need to develop different gimmicks to encourage athletes to give your sport a try or feel good about their participation. In the classroom, we sometimes call these dog-and-pony shows to keep our students' attention. You could run an intramural tournament during your homeroom, before or after school. We promoted a Bring-A-Friend Friday on occasion where non-committed athletes could attend practice with a friend on selected Fridays just to check it out. We also have sponsored holiday parties for our athletes, gone caroling with them, and had an ice-skating party over a holiday break.

If you expect your athletes to commit time to training early in the morning, create a Breakfast Club as a reward for their dedication and cook them breakfast at the end of the training cycle. If you want to promote investment of extra time after a practice to work on additional skills or perfect attendance, create a Guts Club recognizing their achievement at your banquet when they have met your criteria. One of our current head coaches, Eric Olson, randomly assigns girls on his track team to be a secret supporter to learn a little more about her assigned teammate and cheer her on during a meet. Simple acts like these can make a big impact.

I once tried bringing special attention to our varsity wrestlers by posting pictures of our lineup in the lobby and having a drop box where classmates could be part of a Name the Wrestler contest. The names their peers submitted were quite creative, and many were inappropriate for a school setting! You may have a great idea and go to great lengths to make it happen only to find it was not the home run you had hoped for.

Keep trying. As with everything else, you will have to keep brainstorming, reevaluating, and moving forward with new and innovative ideas.

Work hard to promote your own program but also to promote good will within the sporting communities you compete against. For a number of years, my wife would put together sack lunches for our opposing players to eat during their long bus ride home after games. This took some time and resources, but the good will that was built through something so simple was reciprocated for some years to come.

You many also enjoy getting to know the coaches you compete against outside of competition. Our conference wrestling coaches helped build mutual respect by getting together in the springtime at a cookout. Retired head wrestling coach and Hall of Famer Franc Freeman of Bettendorf, Iowa, has been host to a similar social for club level, high school, and collegiate coaches and officials for more than 30 years. It is good food, good camaraderie, and a fun night. I have a great deal of respect for my good friend, former head coach Tom Danner of Western Dubuque, Iowa, who developed a pre-season wrestling social and invites a guest speaker to talk to his parents and supporters to kick off the season. These social events are great ways to listen and learn from your peers while having a good time and a lot of laughs.

There are so many events activities that you can develop to promote and improve your program. These in no way will address the skills, techniques, or conditioning that are critical to performance. They will, though, add an element to your program that can help build a positive atmosphere, which is the essence of building support and enthusiasm. Whether you are working with youth programs, individuals, or teams, work hard in preparation for success but also spend the extra time enriching their experience and enhancing their participation with activities that will foster good will.

GAME DAY

Welcome back to the start of the 2015-2016 school year! In the fall of 1971, I began school for the first time and for the last 44 years, the fall has represented the start of something new. About one-third of that time I was a student, and for two-thirds I have been an educator. It has always been a special time of year for me and although the new year can create a little anxiety about the fear of the unknown, the new challenges and opportunities that lie ahead have always been a source of motivation. I love being in a school setting and really don't know anything else. School has become my home away from home.

I would like to throw out a big challenge to our entire incoming freshman class: GET INVOLVED! I was always looking for a way to become a participant in my school experience and I tried all sorts of activities. Of course, sports became a big part of my life as an athlete and a coach, but there was a time when I tried many other things — band, chorus, swing choir, plays, musicals, FFA, FCA, student government, and other clubs and activities that the school had to offer. Even though you might think the four years ahead of you seem like an eternity, I can tell you firsthand that those years are going to fly by! I have heard it many times before from both our seniors and their parents that they "cannot believe four years are done already." The time will go by quickly and will move even more quickly when you are a participant. When you get involved, you have all sorts of things to look forward to and you will spend more time focused on the pursuit of your goals and dreams. You will not always find that you are good at everything you do, but it is likely you will look back without regret and feel good about how you spent the time with the opportunities presented to you.

Much of life is just that, taking advantage of all of your opportunities and creating your own opportunities by getting involved. Step out of your comfort zone and take some risks to try something new. You won't be great at everything and if you are like me you may not even be good at much of it, but success is not always based on what was achieved. As you get further and further into adulthood, having the self-confidence to try something new can help you travel down that ROAD OF SUCCESS. Earning accolades in your activities can give you a feeling of accomplishment, but the real prize is in developing attitudes that will benefit you down that road.

I've known a lot of former students who blazed that trail of success in all sorts of different areas after leaving school without garnering a bunch of accolades while they were here. That future success was not dependent upon the level of success reached in high school but rather on the great attitudes and work ethic that were developed while pursuing those goals and dreams. By getting involved in a safe environment like high school, you give yourself a chance to develop those critical skills you may need later in life when pursuing something bigger. The next four years of high school can help you solidify the foundation that the great things you pursue later in life will be built upon. Your bonus, on top of being involved in potential life-changing experiences, is that you have the chance to meet some great people along the way and build good friendships that can last a lifetime.

I will also caution you to avoid unnecessary roadblocks. It can be as simple as making good decisions. Life can be challenging enough without creating more obstacles for yourself. Surround yourself with people who inspire you and will be a support system in helping you chase those goals and dreams. There will be plenty of decisions to make as you navigate your way down this road, but in almost every situation there are two paths you can take. And when confronted with the choice between right and wrong, CHOOSE RIGHT!

Participating in risky, dangerous, or even unlawful activities will only delay you in reaching your destination or can potentially take you completely off course. Making bad choices is not a way for you to stand out and certainly not a way to use all your potential. If you really want to do something different, challenge yourself to DO RIGHT. It is very simple: You can never be wrong doing what's right! Stay disciplined and sacrifice the little things in life for the things that REALLY MATTER. You have a great opportunity in front of you and I wish you the best of luck in making your mark. But "luck" is really not the correct word, as it makes your destiny appear out of your control. Don't let life happen to you; go out and make your own luck!

"There are no shortcuts to any place worth going."
—Beverly Sills

CHAPTER 7 ACTIVITIES

- How can you help support the athletes and coaches of other programs at your school?

- Organize a new recruiting activity that you would like to use to encourage athletes at your school to participate in your sport.

- Create a media guide for your program.

- Outline the structure of a quality team banquet.

- Develop another way to highlight or promote the accomplishments of an individual athlete or a team.

Chapter 8

INSIDE YOUR PROGRAM
Little Things Can Make a Big Difference

"Anything you can do, or dream you can, begin it.
Boldness has genius, power, and magic in it."
                                        —*Goethe*

Coach Bob Reade, my Augustana College football coach, shared a poem with his seniors about the importance of "ordinary days" and it has had a great influence on me ever since.

"Don't you kids know that life is made up of ordinary days
When there is no one to pat you on the back?
When there is no one to praise you?
When there is no one to honor you?
When there is no one to see how brave and noble you are?
Almost all of life is made of these ordinary days.
And it is how you live your ordinary days
That determines whether or not you have big moments.
Get out there and make something of your ordinary days."
                                —Ann Kiemel Anderson

Coaches tend to gravitate toward final results and big moments. Make sure to place your focus, though, on the little things that are necessary for success to occur. Your athletes will do the same. The little things are not little at all and collectively will have big impact on your success.

COMMUNICATION

I have heard it mentioned many times in sports that when a team has had great success, it was inevitable considering all the talent that was on the team. In spite of the coaches, the team overcame and won.

Conversely, when a team has played below expectations, the blame is pinned squarely on the coach, disregarding how the athletes may or may not have trained or performed or what the apparent talent level might have been. If that team had only had a better staff, it certainly would have won. You may believe in one or the other concept, but you can't believe in both at the same time: The fact is that winning and losing are a combination of many different factors. When you win it's typically not only the result of player success, and when you lose it is not solely the result of coaching. Both coaches and players alike make contributions to success and failure, and if you are going to win everyone will have to be pulling in the same direction.

I have heard that a philosophy exists in our profession: A coach should take any blame publicly early in the season and then shift criticism to players as the season goes on. I don't subscribe at all to that kind of philosophy or believe in it. That way of thinking might help deflect responsibility short-term by finding someone to blame, but that is not what real leaders do. Calculating who and when to assign blame does not relate well to team building.

There is always a need to identify deficits and there are always things to improve, but assigning blame is not a real action-based solution. When building a team, you are all in it together. There is always plenty of blame to go around for failure, but it is not necessary either early or late in the season to seek out which specific group needs to own it publicly.

128

Part of your unity will be in the development of a system that you believe in. Those "fans" on the periphery of your program will have their own opinions about which system is best, but all you have to do is visit the state championships in your particular sport and you will notice that all sorts of systems rise to the top. It is true you can succeed with any number of approaches, but you must have a belief in what you are doing. That belief must be shared by your players, who will be implementing it.Beyond the belief you have in what you are doing, you have to develop a system in which you have a great depth of knowledge and surround yourself with a knowledgeable staff. Knowledge of program dynamics and interpersonal communication skills is necessary for a coach, but a deep-rooted knowledge in your sport is critical. It is important to have a technical background, knowledge of how to instruct, and an interest in continual growth.

We can be inspired by new information that looks good on paper or sounds intriguing when we hear it explained at a clinic. Lean on your philosophy when deciding to add a new item to your system. You will need to sell it to your coaches and players, teach the fundamental concepts during installation, and correct deficits when the competition has done its part of adjusting to it. Your philosophy will help you decide whether you want to develop more streamlined strategies or expand your strategies with volumes of material.

One thing I strongly suggest doing when you first get into coaching is to acquire the rulebook of your specific sport and read it for understanding. You will find out in a hurry that you really don't have the depth of knowledge of the rules that you initially thought. Rulebooks are detailed and cover all the minutiae of your sport. It is likely you will run into items that you had no idea even existed in there. A deep understanding of your rules makes you a more credible coach when you can recite from memory and communicate that type of detailed information to your athletes. It could make a difference in the heat of battle as well. Officials will certainly recognize a coach who is well versed in the rules.

If you need a better understanding of how little you might actually know about the rules, put on the striped shirt sometime and officiate yourself. Before becoming too critical of an official, make certain you actually know the rules yourself.

That kind of education would serve us all well. I allowed our seniors to officiate at youth tournaments so they could experience the dynamics of officiating. I have had a few opportunities to officiate myself and I found it is not as easy as many of our officials make it look. If you don't believe it, search out an opportunity to officiate and you will understand it much more clearly in short order.

The mechanics and positioning of good officiating can be taxing. When you add all the items you have to anticipate and process, as well as the amount of information you need to have available to make the correct decisions, officiating is a huge job. The pressure is great, because coaches expect it all to be done with perfection.

Because it is so demanding to be a good official, I have a great respect for what officials do. We are fortunate that we have people who are interested in becoming officials and are willing to put themselves in those vulnerable situations.

Of course, they may get it wrong from time to time and unfortunately, there may be a time when their mistake can have a significant impact on the outcome. But I believe that our officials almost always have good intentions. That helps me have some perspective when making my evaluations of their performance. I have found out that looking for the best in people is often a better life philosophy.

From time to time, it is possible that some officials are lacking in integrity, but that is rare and happens in all professions in life, including ours. Most officials officiate for the right reasons and are honorable people. They have a huge responsibility for doing something that is not easy at all.

Developing a positive rapport with the officials can help your cause. When you know the rules and are able to communicate effectively with those who have the final say, they will listen to you a little bit more closely when you have a discussion with them regarding a rule you think may have been misapplied. That will not guarantee they are going to change their call, but they may listen better to what you have to say. Being able to communicate effectively with officials is a key component of long-term success as a coach.

YOUR PLAN

Paying attention to details and communicating effectively will help you develop and implement a plan for your program. If you become a head coach or are allowed to develop your own plan as a coach of a lower level, you will spend a great deal of time planning. Your plan will include off-season and in-season strength and conditioning plans, speed and agility plans, yearlong guide, season outline, weekly shell, practice plans, game plans, as well as individual drill period plans that you will use when instructing athletes. Spending the necessary time in making organized, detailed, and effective plans is one of the most important skills in coaching and your program.

If you are a head coach at any level, put a great deal of time into planning your practices. You may like a more detailed practice plan with all the periods scripted, or you may be able to operate with a more basic shell. Whatever works for you, make sure you give any assistants you are working with plenty of time to look it over and plan for their own responsibilities. Use technology and online resources to enhance your plan and to communicate your plan to other coaches on staff.

You may want to develop a consistent routine at practice so your athletes clearly understand the flow, making your time spent together more efficient. You might develop a weekly routine where you cover certain aspects of game planning on specific days before your competition.

Or your philosophy may be better served by creating more variation during a practice or during the week. Regardless of what general type of practice you utilize, make sure your plan is well thought out and fits your philosophy.

There are a lot of practice variations out there that you could incorporate if you want to vary your plan from time to time. Use Sudden Change practices, where you script out game-like situations, forcing your athletes to change gears as they would during a game.

131

Central Football Practice Schedule   Date: 9-7-11   Team: ANAMOSA

videotaped (Y)/ n   clock y / n ○

Best D/O Player: #54
Schemes:
TH/LT

TIME	PERIOD	Kreiter	Streets	Foxen	Birt	Sikkema	LaKose	Lansing	Block	Lubben	Meyer
3:20	Pre-practice Drills	VLB vs. RB	DB vs. TE	PK	FSLB vs. RB	FSDB vs. TE	OL T.O.L.	QB	DL	QB	TE
3:35	Positive Wednesday FG										
3:40	Stretching	x Captains	x			x		x			
3:55											
3:55	O Skills	Skills	VRB	Frames	VTE Stalk	FS Frames	FSOL	VQB	OL	VQB	FSTE
4:10	Full 7 on 7 (Blitz)				vs. 9th		vs. 10th				
4:30	D Drill	WLB &	I/S /Run	VDB	FSILB	FSC	FSDL	FSS	I/S /Run	VC	VLB
4:45	M Green I/S Run	RE w/DL	w/DL						w/LB		
4:45	Special Teams	W - Punt & PR vs. Sophs									
5:00											
5:00	Team Offense CLOSED OPEN	Situational On "2" /FG									
5:30	Team Defense Script:	Situational D - Live Goalline 5 Plays									
5:50	Champions	"Even as we dream, we begin to succeed... even as we succeed, we begin to dream."									

ANNOUNCEMENTS
1. Highlight
2. KROS
3. Lifting !
4. Big Stick - Popcorn
5. Leadership Team
6. $ / t-shirts

Video Review:

Above is a sample practice plan that I have used in the past. There is nothing special about it except it worked well within the framework of how we wanted to conduct our practice.

Develop a Positive Practice where athletes and coaches enhance their normal routine by commenting on positive things that teammates and coaches do at practice.

132

There is also a Nascar Practice, which is a variation in speed or tempo of a certain aspect of practice. We called it Tempo Tuesday. We also implemented a Red Flag Practice, which was handed down by my great mentor and former head wrestling and Hall of Fame Coach Jeff Newmeister. It was an abbreviated but intense practice, which addressed more the mental aspect of competition when athletes become fatigued.

As a staff, plan ahead and brainstorm unique situations that you can incorporate into your practice that could potentially occur during a game. Add a "rules of the game" period to your schedule where you in-service your athletes as to special situations or specific rules. As a head football coach, I once had an assistant who was good about bringing up obscure but potentially important situations that we might encounter during a game.

As an example, early in the season during a quarterfinal run we had a big matchup with a traditional power. Late in the game, we had to decide whether our best option to win would be taking a snap during a punting situation or walking out of the end zone to take a safety. Although it was a calculated risk, our coaching staff had made sure that prior to that game we had reviewed that same situation during a pre-season practice. Because of that, it was not a stressful decision during a tense moment.

I have seen a less detailed, handwritten practice plan from head wrestling and Hall of Fame Coach Dan Mashek, who is the all-time win leader in Iowa high school wrestling history. How the practice looks on paper is not nearly as important as the content, flow, and your ability to instruct and motivate your players during your time together.

Planning for individual drill periods is the nuts and bolts of your operation. Put a great deal of effort into developing drills that will directly affect your players' performance. Use film study to identify areas of improvement that need to be addressed. If you are able, film practice sessions and provide feedback to your athletes or use other clips to model the type of performance you are looking for. Make sure that your practice plans match the skills that your athletes will use during competition.

Don't necessarily believe clinic drills that sound really good in theory are always the answer. They may look really cool but don't always serve a real value in trying to teach the concepts you feel are important to your athletes. Develop muscle memory by mirroring the fundamentals you want to see during performance with those you are instructing in practice.

You may find one of the more challenging aspects of coaching athletics is creating a bridge between practice skills and competition. Your young and average players will have a more difficult time transferring what they do in practice to game situations, but repetition of fundamentals is a key component to success.

Break down complex skills and teach various aspects in a sequential manner. Our daughter, Haley, was a competitive gymnast through much of her youth. I was always amazed to see the progression her coaches would use in the development of a complex movement through the instruction of its fundamental parts. Through a step-by-step progression, she could master an elaborate skill that was the sum of the collective parts. Because of that process, gymnasts are able to make difficult movements look easy.

There are many resources you might explore for discovering new drills and skills that will match the fundamentals and skills you want to teach. Clinics, online resources, and books are all great places to start. Visit your local college programs and take advantage of coaches who may have many things to offer you. They are typically accommodating and gracious in helping you develop your plan.

There is not a better coach in the country at running an organized summer camp than head wrestling Coach Dave Mitchell of Luther College, Decorah, Iowa, along with his assistant coach, Jeff O'Gara. During the many years we brought teams to participate in his camp, he was always great at providing coaches with helpful information about how to build a program and insight into how he ran his. Our nephew Justin Kreiter was a national runner-up, 2X All-American and Academic All-American in their wrestling program and I cannot speak highly enough about the first-class program they provided for him and all their athletes to reach their goals.

Don't be afraid to develop your own drills. Use your own knowledge and background to create drills that fit well into your system. We end up searching for and using a great deal of information from other sources, but sometimes we fail to remember we ourselves have a lot to offer. Part of the fun in coaching is developing your own briefcase full of materials. From time to time, those items that you create may be identified as being innovative and forward-thinking and used by others.

Make sure you dedicate a great deal of time to develop your plan. Nothing is more unprofessional than coaches who show up unprepared or simply wing it when they get there. You may have a lot of knowledge rattling around in your brain, but without a plan it is just knowledge. Show up on time, which should entail arriving early, having a concrete plan in writing, and taking full advantage of your scheduled time coaching with energy and enthusiasm.

When you are first getting acclimated to coaching, during practice you may need to over-plan your drill periods. It will take some time for you to gain the experience you need to estimate how much material you can get through during a specific practice period. You may also spend a lot of time planning for the first day only to come away with the feeling that things did not go as planned. For both the new and more experienced coaches alike, it may take a while to get into the natural flow and rhythm of practice that develops over time.

Young coaches seem to rush through material a little more quickly because they don't necessarily have the background to embellish each item covered. Make sure you have more material than what you think you might need so you don't end up scrambling to avoid dead time during practice.

Remember that quality is more important than quantity. Experienced coaches may run into the opposite problem and not get through all the material they would like. They have a tendency to elaborate, which can certainly enhance the presentation but may take up much valuable time in the process.

Utilize pre-practice time to think through the logistics of your drills and ensure you have all the equipment you may need ready to go. Have a detailed plan listing what you want to cover and how you will instruct the skill so the period will flow from one activity to the next. Make sure you check for understanding during your instruction. If you are able to, utilize pre-practice or post-practice meetings with your players to reinforce what you are teaching. The mental aspect of instruction including the use of film can really enhance the physical work. Film does not lie, so it can be a great way to evaluate an athlete's performance.

Find ways to develop mental toughness in your athletes by challenging them physically. Most athletes won't welcome strenuous conditioning, but they will appreciate having an edge over their opponents because of it. Conditioning is not a punishment but a reward, so that when you are in a tough competition you know you are in superior shape and you will be confident in your ability to persevere.

By educating yourself on techniques of proper conditioning and training, you can push your athletes without putting them in danger of risking injury. Be careful not to over-train, which could have the opposite effect if athletes are hurt in the process. Always keep the health and safety of your athletes the highest priority when planning practice.

Have a preconceived plan for varying the intensity of conditioning coordinated with your competition schedule. When should you maximize conditioning? When do you want to back off? When will it be necessary to train through competition? When do you need to peak? As you develop more experience as a coach, you will find it easier to understand when to implement the different periods of training and be able to judge your team as to their needs.

On the next page is the fitness test we used during our seasons called the 12-minute test. Have your athletes work with a partner so while one is performing the test, the other is keeping score. This is run with a continuous clock, and the partner reports scores to the coaches or managers who act as recorders during the rest periods. This was a rugby fitness test I experienced as an athlete and adapted to our programs. There are many other fitness tests you can use as benchmarks or challenges to your teams.

12-MINUTE TEST

TIME	ACTIVITY	POINTS
6 minutes	run 10 yards	2 pts. down/back
1 minute	Rest	
1 minute	push-ups	1 pt. each
30 seconds	Rest	
1 minute	sit-ups	1 pt. each
30 seconds	Rest	
45 seconds	up-down	1 pt. each
30 seconds	Rest	
45 seconds	4-count burpie	1 pt. each

Athletes were not excited about performing the 12-Minute test, but over the years, our real competitors used it as a means of challenging themselves. We used the philosophy of "work hard and play hard" as we would follow the test by having a watermelon feed if we were outdoors or eating popsicles from time to time when we were indoors.

Besides planning practices, you will also need to plan for the length of your season and create an outline for your entire year. This will involve a great deal of foresight and advanced planning. This plan will serve as a guide for you to accomplish important tasks at the appropriate times during your season and the year. Of course, you may need to modify your long-term plan because of the many factors that cause us to adjust over time.

Your plan should align with your philosophy, though, and help you accomplish your goals. Don't forget to incorporate leadership training into your plan.

As a head coach, you will be responsible for having thought through everything that needs to be done each day, week, season, and year. Use your staff's input and delegate tasks as you see fit. The following questions are a small sampling of what you will need to think about prior to the start of your season:

- Have you communicated with your athletic secretary and athletic director, supplying them with rosters and making sure that all your athletes have met eligibility requirements?

- Do all athletes have all forms on file? Are all prerequisites met regarding health screening?
- Where and how will you stretch?
- How long will your practice last? How do you plan on staying on time?
- How will you deal with poor weather? Is there an alternative location if you move indoors?
- Who will be responsible for setting up your field or taking out equipment?
- Where are the medical supplies? How will you deal with injuries or medical emergencies?
- Is there a schedule set up for each location? Are practice times set up for each level in your program?
- What are your lettering criteria?
- Have you inventoried your equipment? Have you
- ordered the needed equipment or supplies?
- How will you adjust the intensity and load of strength training in relation to competition and the length of your season?
- What sequential order do you use in the implementation of schemes during the season? Does that volume change during various times of the year?
- Are there significant holiday breaks or educational checkpoints where training will need to be adjusted?
- Have you taken care of accommodations for overnight trips?
- How will you manage your budget?

Certain sports will require a great deal of time in scrutinizing your game plan. When you are an assistant, you may be required to do a considerable amount of work in scouting opponents and charting their tendencies. Go above and beyond the call of duty and be detail-oriented when developing your specific plan. Think through all the things you might encounter and be prepared to tackle the things you didn't anticipate. This will require a big effort. Be willing to take on new responsibilities and work with your head coaches to relieve them of some tasks so they can more efficiently deal with the additional administrative duties of their position. Create a clearly defined depth chart and have contingency plans in case of injuries.

When you are the head coach, your selection of quality and knowledgeable assistant coaches will pay dividends. It is a challenge to bring a group of young people together to work as a championship team; it is an altogether different challenge, but critical to success, that you develop a cohesive plan that will defeat an opponent. Be prepared to devote a great amount of time to game planning. The more time you spend becoming familiar with each other as well as with your opponent, the easier it will be to make adjustments during a game.

Use the strengths of all your coaches to help define their role in planning for game day and the implementation of your plan during the event. Give them the direction and resources they need to be successful. Have high expectations for them but give them ownership in the process, as it will help develop pride and loyalty in your program.

You are ultimately responsible, so be engaged in all aspects of your program and intervene when necessary. Direct, oversee, and evaluate but do not micromanage.

There are many things you need to think about prior to your competition. This list of questions just scratches the surface of what you will need to think about in game planning:

- Do you have a clearly defined depth chart and have contingency plans in case of injuries?
- Have you communicated with transportation about the vehicles needed and departure and return times? Do you have a bus list?
- Do your secretaries have your team list with departure times?
- Have your parents been informed about the bus times and location of events?
- Do you have contact information and needed medical forms?

- Have you delegated responsibilities such as putting together an extra equipment bag, uniforms, video equipment, and additional equipment you will need for the games?
- Do you have all the stat sheets and training equipment ready?
- Have you communicated with all your support staff about their responsibilities and travel plans?
- Have you packed the water bottles?

When your individuals or teams advance to state events, make sure you have detailed itineraries available for your athletes and their parents with all the contact information they might need. Think through your timeline, which includes: Where and when will you train? How will you transport to the event? When and where will meals fit into the itinerary? Where will you lodge and what are the room assignments, curfews, and expectations? Is laundry available? How will you use downtime? What are the plans for keeping up with academics? You will want your entire focus to be on performance, so having a well-thought-out plan will allow you to put your energies and focus into competition.

Place a great emphasis on your planning and you will find that things will run more efficiently. It all seems like a lot of work, but once you get a system set in place and start your routines, much of this will become just a normal part of what you do. What will certainly end up taking more time and causing more mental anguish is the turmoil you will encounter if you are unorganized. If you are not a naturally organized person, become organized so you will become an effective coach. Make sure that all of your planning reflects your vision. All those you lean on to put into effect your plan should be on the same page as you.

Sun Tzu once said about preparation for battle, "Victorious warriors win first and then go to war, while defeated warriors go to war first and then seek to win."

OFF-SEASON

The amount of time committed to your program during off-season is where our profession has changed most dramatically over the years. Although we are always planning for the future to some extent, I never thought the next season began until our end-of-the-season banquet was over. Beyond your ongoing training efforts, use the off-season to evaluate your program and players. You will also organize opportunities to allow athletes to continue to develop their skills.

Off-season will be the time when your individuals and teams will make the most significant gains during strength and conditioning phases as well as in speed and agility. There are a lot of great programs for you to use, or if you are well versed in the concepts of strength and conditioning, you could develop your own program. It will continuously evolve as you gain more knowledge and tap into all the great resources available to you in developing your approach. Make your efforts in this area a priority.

You will want a format that creates unity in what you do. There are a lot of program formats that will be beneficial to your athletes, although some will be more physiologically sound or better suited to your needs than others.

But the mental approach, personal commitment, and can-do attitudes that develop can far outweigh the physical gains made during training and applied to competition. This is a great time to develop physically, but it is also a great time to develop leadership and build unity and momentum toward the upcoming season.

As a head coach of multiple sports that occurred in back-to-back seasons, I had a different perspective on how skill development should fit into our overall athletic program. I preferred that our athletes participate and compete in another sport as often as possible. I was convinced we could develop competitors through competition! Encourage your student-athletes to explore other areas of interest and urge them to get involved in leadership opportunities. Stay in contact with them so you can monitor their academic progress.

After our football season, we had a draft night where our junior leaders would draft all players in our program onto leadership teams for a points challenge. It was a great opportunity for our players to lead the developing student-athletes. Team leaders of each group were responsible for serving as mentors for members of their group and encouraged them to make good choices during the off-season.

A point system was used in awarding points for activities in three categories. There was high value placed on academic achievement, leadership, and participation in other activities. Group leaders wanted to draft players who possessed qualities beyond that of performance during the season.

We made our No. 1 draft choice selections at each grade level a well-publicized event. It typically served to reinforce the type of players we wanted to develop in our programs with strengths in all three areas. Points were awarded for participation or achievement in subcategories, which included things like semester grades and school leadership positions. This was a great way to support our athlete's positive efforts for self-improvement. When integrating a similar system, you could deduct points from the group total for anything that could negatively impact the team such as failing grades or inappropriate conduct, if that reflected your philosophy.

There will be many other off-season opportunities for your athletes to improve their skills, but always remember to be cognizant of the in-season sports and be respectful of your athlete's free time and family or work commitments. Also, make sure you are aware of and follow your state's off-season contact rules.

The off-season will be the time to get your coaching staff together and evaluate all aspects of your program. Do advance scouting of your future opponents. Review past film and scout your own team for areas where change is needed and the areas you would like to enhance. It is also the time of year you will want to sit down with your coaches and athletes individually and do goal-setting activities with them. Organize clinic opportunities for your staff and camps for your team.

We were always looking for new ways to elevate our program to the next level. At one point, I worked with my former Head Wrestling Coach Jeff Newmeister and his assistant, my brother, Eugene, at the

North Scott School District in Eldridge, Iowa, to organize a freestyle wrestling club shared between both our communities. We reached out and invited other area programs to join us in an attempt to create an environment in which coaches could send their athletes to wrestle and get better without the concern of being unethically recruited by another school. The organization was run under the guidelines of USA Wrestling and was a great opportunity for wrestlers to get together in a non-school yet competitive setting. At the time, there were not too many similar opportunities in the area, so it was beneficial for everyone involved. Today, many programs have developed their own similar organizations, so those opportunities are not as unique as they once were.

Off-season opportunities in football involved skills and drills during the summer months after morning strength and conditioning. There were organized 7-on-7 team opportunities with neighboring schools and attendance at team camps, as well as individual and prospect camps. These are typical activities today for all programs, but not that many years ago many of these activities would have made your program stand out from the rest. Today, these are all expected components of the things you do, even though it is unlikely these extra agendas will include compensation for your invested time. Be prepared to get involved, regardless of pay. That is what coaches do.

Just as you need to maintain an element of fun in your youth organizations, you should also try to have a little fun in the off-season as well with your older athletes. It is easy to find drills that will add an element of fun and be highly competitive. Sometimes our athletes don't realize they are developing valuable skills while they are having a good time.

As a former rugby player, I would often incorporate Touch 7's in our summer conditioning program. It was a great conditioning tool as well as an opportunity to work on form tackling in a controlled, non-contact situation. Our athletes enjoyed being introduced to a unique sport and over the years we had many young men and women go on to play that great game of rugby at the collegiate and club level after leaving high school.

Use the off-season to organize your storage area, order new equipment and take inventory. Work with your athletic director and Booster Club in making requests for items you will need the following year. Keep your administration aware of things that are happening in your program and share significant items with your school board.

Many colleges will use the off-season to contact you to fill out information about potential prospects. Consider putting together a standard form with information about each prospect that will enhance any video you provide to recruiters. Here is a sample form I have used in the past:

Individual Player Profile: Name (Grade)
Home Phone: / Cell Phone:

Address

DeWitt, IA 52742

Football

2010	RB / DC	2009	RB / DC (Varsity)	2008	RB / DB (Sophomore)	2007	RB / DB (Freshman)
	Varsity Captain		Defensive Starter / Letterman		52 carries/573 yards / 9 TD		
	2 Way Starter / 2X Letterman		19 Tackles		12 tackles		
	91 carries/979 yards / 10 TD				10.3 KOR average		
	10 Tackles / 1 INT						
	First Team All-District						

Height	6'1"		6' 0"		5' 10"		5' 10"
Weight	185		170 lbs.		155 lbs.		145 lbs.
40 yard	4.67 (Hand Timed)		4.84		4.95		5.03
VJ	30.5		25		25		19

**Outstanding Punt Returner*

Wrestling (Winter)	Track (Spring)	Baseball (Summer)	Academics/Leadership
2007-08	**2008**	**2008**	**2008**
JV	JV	Freshman Team	3.33 Cum GPA
24-10 145 lbs.	100/200 Dash	.380 Avg.	
		15 Stolen Bases	
2008-09	**2009**	**2009**	**2009**
Letterman	Letterman	JV Team	3.42 Cum GPA
20-11 152 lbs.	4th Place All-Conference 100 Meter	.375 Avg.	2 Semester Honor Roll
		20 Stolen Bases	
2009-10	**2010**	**2010**	**2010**
2X Letterman	2X Letterman	DNP	3.47 Cum GPA
2nd Place All-Conference	Captain		2 Semester Honor Roll
25-6 160 lbs.	2nd Place All-Conference 100 Meter		Student Council Representative
	State Qualifier Class 3A 100 Meter		
2010-11	**2011**	**2011**	**2011**
Team Captain	3X Letterman	DNP	3.55 Cum GPA
3X Letterman	2X Captain		2 Semester Honor Roll
Conference Champion	Conference Champion 100 Meter		Student Council Vice-President
4th Place Class 2A IHSAA	Drake Relay Qualifier		27 ACT Score
32-4 171 lbs.	2nd Place IHSAA Class 3A 100 Meter		

Your off-season will also be the off-season for coaches at the collegiate level. You will start to see increased activity in recruiting at your school. Their visits are something you should embrace and be thankful for. It is a great honor for your athletes when coaches provide them an opportunity to continue their education while competing at their institution. Be truthful in your evaluation and recommendation of your players. If you use some false advertising in trying to promote a player, that inaccurate portrayal could lead to a lack of trust. A spoiled relationship could have long-term ramifications for future athletes in your program. Build an honest relationship with them, as they can provide an invaluable service to your athletes and their parents.

Over the years of speaking with college coaches, I have come to the conclusion that quality programs are looking for three things. First, they want to know if your athletes are young people of high character because if they are not, they will be a detriment to their program. Second, they are looking for individuals who can make it academically at their institution. If they cannot, it would be a poor investment by them, as they will not make it in the end. Last, they are evaluating the talent and measurable qualities that allow athletes to compete at their specific level and fill a need the college has. Our athletes may think these qualities are evaluated in reverse order, but there is a lot of talent out there, so they should spend their energies strengthening the first two in order to give themselves a chance.

In my final season as a head football coach, we had a substantial number of recruiters representing all levels of college football contact our school about players in our program. It took a big effort to have information available for our prospects and spend the time with each one of them. It was not a contractual obligation, but I always saw a dual benefit. Having our athletes compete at the next level not only helped them in the pursuit of academic and athletic goals, but also served as a great tool in showcasing for our younger athletes what was possible while participating in our program.

I still enjoy talking to coaches of those programs when they visit our school, as they are like-minded and have a great passion for their programs and the coaching profession.

GAME DAY

A few Sundays ago was both a great day and sad moment at our house. Super Bowl Sunday is the culmination of the football season that started in early August and this event makes it a great day for me. The sad moment is to think I have to wait another five months before it all starts again. Jenny does not feel the same way about all the football I watch, and sees Super Bowl Sunday as the end of a torturous seven months when I have football playing every chance I get. Haley has joked that my epitaph will read: "Here lies a man who loved football!" I was born in 1965, so I have been on the planet for all 50 games although the game itself is just another exciting football game for me. I can't say that the Bronco-Panther matchup was anything special, although the team I was rooting for did win the game. I like to read and listen to all the pre-game preparatory hype that builds up to the game, and I often end up rooting for the underdog for some reason. In the end, regardless of all the prognosticators, one team ends up getting the job done. In sports there is an old saying that rings true over and over again: YOU GET WHAT YOU EARN!

One of the cruel realities of sports is that in the end the scoreboard or scorecard determines who is pronounced the victor. You can find ways to justify, blame, explain, or rationalize a loss, but the scoreboard does not lie. Those who experience the agony of defeat have to face that reality. Keeping both victory and defeat in perspective is important in sports, and in life as far as that goes. Sometimes you are going to be the victor, and sometimes you will have to face the adversity of losing. That can be okay, too. Coaches and athletes prepare for competition to win and you had better develop a winning mindset before you step into the competitive arena. If not, it is likely you don't have the focus necessary to compete and win. Becoming mentally prepared for competition can be as important as getting physically ready for an event. Your brain can be a great ally or it can be an adversary. If you have prepared the right way both mentally and physically, having to deal with loss can be one of the best ways to bounce back from defeat, reevaluate, and get a lot better. So a loss can certainly be used as a learning tool.

Sometimes you lose because your opponent was physically or technically better than you. Team dynamics also plays a role. That is what team leadership training and team development are all about, what all teams are working toward. It requires constant evaluation and honestly, just a lot of hard work. If team leadership is lacking, attitudes can get in the way, and if individuals are not willing to sacrifice and commit to the cause, then the best-

146

made plans can go to waste. There is no shame in losing if you have done all the right things in preparation. If you have made good choices, trained, committed, sacrificed, and believed in yourself and your teammates — and have given it everything you have got — in the end you will not have regrets knowing you did all you could. If not, you may always have some lingering questions.

That being said, losing still hurts. We hosted the district wrestling tournament, and I happened to be out in the lobby when I heard a familiar loud bang I recognized from years past. Sure enough, near that commotion was a young man drenched in sweat who was in agony as he moved about our atrium. He had thrown his headgear into a custodial cart, thus the loud sound, and he now wandered in the atrium making the agonizing moans of someone who had just experienced a form of grief known only to those who had done all the right things but still came up short.

I recognized all of those sounds because I have lived them in the past. As a senior in high school I lost my state-qualifying match 3-2 in overtime, preventing a trip to the state tournament. In college I came up short again, also by way of a 3-2 overtime loss that would have given me All-American status. Both matches were devastating and seemed even worse because in the sport of wrestling it is an individual loss and there are fewer places to look to assess blame. It is you and you alone. The loss is compounded because the sacrifices you have to make in that sport can be extreme. There was a time that the heartache seemed like something I would never be able to bounce back from, but history shows in my case that even when I get knocked down a few times, I'm going to keep getting back up. Cruel lessons taught through adversity create resiliency.

Although my heart went out to that young man in our lobby who was devastated by the loss, I know that time and perspective will turn that negative into something that will strengthen his character for a lifetime.

"Work Will Win When Wishing Won't."
—Todd Blackledge

147

CHAPTER 8 ACTIVITIES

- Create a sample practice plan for your sport.

- Assemble a list of drills you will use in sequence when teaching skills to your athletes.

- Make a list of conditioning drills with varying intensity to be used during your different periods of training.

- Develop a list of items you will need to make sure to cover during the pre-season and prior to games as part of your planning.

- Outline the activities you think are necessary to organize during your off-season.

Chapter 9

BEYOND THE SCOREBOARD
What It Is All About

When things go wrong, as they sometimes will,
When the road you're trudging seems all uphill,
When funds are low and the debts are high,
And you want to smile but you have to sigh,
When care is pressing you down a bit,
Rest if you must, but don't you quit.
Life is queer with its twists and turns,
As every one of us sometimes learns,
And many a failure turns about,
When he might have won if he'd stuck it out.
Don't give up, though the pace seems slow —
You may succeed with another blow.
Often the goal is nearer than
It seems to a faint and faltering man;
Often the struggler has given up
When he might have captured the victor's cup,
And he learned too late, when the night slipped down,
How close he was to the golden crown.
Success is failure turned inside out —
The silver tint of the clouds of doubt,
And you never can tell how close you are —
It may be near when it seems afar;
So stick to the fight when you're hardest hit —
It's when things seem worst that you mustn't quit.

—Author Unknown

One of my great mentors in coaching was Hall of Fame Wrestling Coach Jeff Tampir of Maquoketa, Iowa. As an aspiring head coach, I learned a great deal from him about building a program, leadership, and handling young people. He had an exceptional coaching career, and he was also an excellent classroom teacher. He was an outstanding coach, but what made his career unique was that he himself never wrestled as a competitor.

He once told me his story of becoming inspired to coach the sport of wrestling when he was a college student. One evening, someone convinced him to accompany him to watch a young wrestler from Iowa State University wrestle on the campus of the University of Northern Iowa. After watching the young man by the name of Dan Gable wrestle, he was so inspired he knew he wanted to become a wrestling coach.

You don't have to have an extensive background in your sport or have been an exceptional athlete yourself to become a great coach. Few know that legendary University of Kentucky basketball Coach Adolph Rupp got his start in coaching in Marshalltown, Iowa, where he led their wrestling team to a state title in 1926. Great coaches are often great teachers and possess the qualities that are necessary to foster in others success that has nothing to do with their own personal history.

I do think some coaches have natural abilities that make them well suited for this profession. The best could coach any sport and have success. I don't think those skills are innate, though. Regardless of what skills you have or are lacking, I believe you are able to learn the new skills that will help you improve and get better. The key is that you are trying.

Don't be that coach who puts on a certain personality when his individuals or team is doing well and quickly turns his back on them when things go in the opposite direction. Don't become that coach whom people want to tune out as soon as he starts talking. Athletes are not inspired through fear and intimidation or demeaning language. Some coaches seem to talk only so they can hear themselves speak. Others tend to point out the obvious during hard times but don't offer any real solutions.

Generally speaking, most of us grow tired of the coach who is habitually critical, regularly negative, and quick to point out our deficits and place blame. I often think it is actually a built-in protective mechanism to mask their own low self-confidence. Criticism is a necessary tool to initiate self-improvement, but when it is not balanced with optimism it can have the opposite affect. Athletes are not inspired through fear and intimidation. It is important that you are able to deliver the important message without having it get lost because of the delivery.

We tend to tune out the presenter when our perceptions are telling us, "Here he goes again." Athletes and coaches alike want to be inspired and lifted up by their leaders. They are also looking for more solution-based discussions and less ranting. Listening to a regular complainer gets old in a hurry. Learning how to communicate effectively will help you deliver the most important information. Recognize your own strengths and weaknesses in this area and work hard to become a great communicator while inspiring youth.

Show enthusiasm around your athletes and learn to be nurturing. Make sure you actually take the time to listen during times when you might have thought to speak. Become a great leader who is consistent in your approach with youth and not dependent on the scoreboard. Become the respected mentor to whom others want to entrust their children. Take pride in this great profession because you have the ability to change young people's lives. Coaching is a special fraternity and you will share many common experiences with coaches of all different sports. You may develop closer bonds and friendships with other coaches over time because they are people who understand what our profession is all about. In social situations, you may find you spend less time talking about other people's careers and more time talking about the teams and athletes you coach. You will certainly love talking about both topics, even though there are times when you will want to be away from it all.

I've asked many coaches over the years what things they liked most about coaching and what they disliked. In almost every case, the most enjoyable part was the relationship with their athletes. The most frustrating aspects were bus rides, equipment check-in, or parent interactions. All three of them are not likely to change, so get used to them. They come with the territory.

Watching players have to deal with injuries is also one of the disappointing aspects of athletics, an unfortunate result of competition. It feels even worse when that injury prevents an athlete's return, especially as an upperclassman. But when we make the choice to participate, those are the risks we take. We never fully know when participation in athletics is going to come to an end but it is inevitable. One of the reasons we place such a heavy emphasis on our athlete's education is that when an athlete's participation does come to an end, it does not make a difference. It is their education that is going to make so many more opportunities for them.

I always felt more disheartened when an athlete quit not because of injuries, but because quitting seemed to be the only alternative to frustration or disappointment. The opportunity to change an athlete's perspective or outlook is one of the important reasons we should encourage him to stay involved. Beyond their importance to the team, when athletes quit they miss out on valuable life lessons and experiences they stand to learn through participation. Athletics is not the only way to develop the skills necessary for life, but little will be gained by quitting. I have found it difficult to convince young people to change their mind once that decision was made.

It would often take me quite some time to move forward after a young person had quit, knowing he might later regret making that decision. I have learned over the years to make sure to listen to these athletes in a nonjudgmental way, wish them good luck, and let them know I would always be available to them if they ever needed my help in the future. Making a change in my attitude helped me deal with that disappointment and also left me in a better position to maintain a good relationship with a young person I still might potentially serve as a mentor.

Be thoughtful when making a decision about promoting any athlete or your own child to a higher level. You don't want to deny them an opportunity they deserve, but you also don't want to put them in a position where they will be under unnecessary scrutiny or struggle with peer relationships because of it. In reality, if it involves your own children, their performance will need to be so outstanding that there is no question why those decisions were made. If not, it could spark a storm of unnecessary controversy.

Put the same amount of thought into your decisions to move lower-level athletes up to a higher level, as making those decisions could have program-wide consequences. You may have an easier time doing this when the sport uses objective criteria to evaluate performance rather than an assessment that is subjective. Upperclassmen who are passed over so that younger athletes can fill their roles may not respond positively, creating potential team issues. Moving them up may be the correct decision, but just be aware there could be unwanted, unintended costs you will have to deal with if you are going to make those moves successfully.

You might consider making those kinds of changes later in the season after giving those who had committed to your program for a longer period of time an early opportunity. Waiting to promote an athlete could serve two beneficial roles by first allowing the upperclassmen a chance to prove what he could or could not do while also creating a clear public perception of why your move was necessary. There are athletes from time to time who are so skilled it would be unfair not to elevate them immediately.

You will encounter some critics who are not supportive of your decisions and others who hope to see you fail. You have to have a thick skin to become a coach. At times it may feel like there are some who look to find fault in all that you do. Some of these critics may accuse you of having forgotten how to coach. Of course, that will happen when you are not having success. The good news is that you can reinvent yourself very quickly without doing much of anything but winning!

There will never be enough in this profession. You will never have enough success. Your team will never have reached the pinnacle often enough. You will always be striving for something more. You may also find that the losses may end up having a bigger impact on you than the wins. Winning may give you some deep sense of satisfaction, but tough losses will stick with you for a long time. It is amazing how much your happiness may hinge upon a bunch of adolescent kids! Understand that when your hopes and dreams are linked to a 17-year old or younger, things are not always going to go very well from time to time.

Some have likened coaching to an abusive, self-destructive disease. If your goals are to become a fulltime coach, you will invest a great deal of time and energy in your coaching. If your coaching duties are on top of your teaching responsibilities, you will still invest a great deal of time in coaching.

I estimated that I put in an additional 30 to 40 hours a week beyond my teaching duties while coaching two sports. Add to that the time and energy to be a successful classroom teacher, and even more time and energy to be a good spouse and parent.

But it is all worth it. I can be at peace with the results of my efforts in the classroom and as a coach, knowing I made a commitment and worked to the best of my abilities. I have been a person of integrity and tried to make a positive impact on young people.

As important as teaching and coaching were to me, though, my role and responsibilities as a husband and father trumped both careers. Your athletic endeavors cannot be your life and your career cannot define who you are. Your legacy goes much deeper than your coaching credentials and the impact you have made while pursuing your goals and dreams.

Those who don't really know you may have the perception that your life mission is all about winning and losing, but make sure that is just a perception. Make your life more meaningful than that. I am not saying that you will not put your heart and soul into competition in the pursuit of excellence. Winning is important. I love to win and I love what victory feels like. But when it is all over, if all you can account for is your record, then you really did not take advantage of the real opportunities in your life.

I had someone inquire once as to what kind of legacy I would want to leave. After thinking about it, I know my true legacy is easily defined. It is my children. Coaching and teaching pale in comparison to our family name and the ability of our children to carry on our family legacy with pride.

Your family will also have a unique experience living a life surrounded by the coaching profession. There may be times where you will have to sacrifice watching your own kids participate because you will be coaching other parents' children somewhere else. Make sure you think this through before making a commitment, as you will not want to regret missing their activities when it is all over.

My wife, Jenny, did not miss an event. I did miss a few things over the years so I relished the time I did get to be around my son, Casey, at practice and competition when he finally got to high school. I did not get to have the same experience with my daughter, Haley, as I did not coach any of the sports in which she participated. We did get to spend some great times together when she helped out on Friday nights with football stats, and over the years we spent some great times together with sports. She was totally engaged in our coaching lifestyle, my biggest supporter, and enjoyed the fact that her dad was a coach. She was probably the most disappointed one when I stepped down as a coach.

You also need to recognize when your discussion of practice or competition is appropriate at home and when everyone has had enough. For sure, your family will have to be "all in" when it comes to embracing this profession. Because it will affect family time and may be a topic of discussion outside the home, you have to know when it's time to shift your focus on coaching to something else.

If you don't develop a balance, you could force everyone to live your job 24-7. Letting your priorities get out of alignment can be a recipe for disaster.

Coaching your own son or daughter will be a unique situation and one you will want to handle delicately so that it becomes a gratifying one. I did not start coaching for the specific intentions of coaching my own children but built programs that I hoped they would someday be proud to be a part of and find some success. At the youth level, coaching your own children will be better accepted since many of those assistants are often volunteers. If you take on paid or volunteer

155

positions at a higher level, there will be the perception that your involvement is strictly to influence your own child's participation.

Although you will maintain the same standards and expectations for your son or daughter that you would for their teammates, be aware that your relationship with them will be viewed differently and actually be different. It only makes sense since the depth of your relationship with your child goes so much deeper. Some may second-guess any of your decisions regarding your child, whether you are handing out discipline or recognizing accomplishments. Regardless, embrace the experience of coaching your child.

Sports have always been a special part of my life, but when I was a 17-year-old, my future in sports became uncertain. In the spring of my junior year in high school, I was diagnosed with testicular cancer. It was quite a shock and today, as a father, I have a better appreciation of what my parents must have gone through at that time. In my youthful mind, though, I was most concerned about not getting a chance to play baseball that summer. Head Coach Randy Denner of North Scott School District, Eldridge, Iowa, assured me that when I returned the next year I could catch all of the doubleheaders, but he advised me to put all my energy into fighting the disease. He was certainly a nurturing coach and helped me deal with some of my initial fears at a time I needed it the most.

Of course, that summer I learned that not playing baseball was the least of my worries. One of my real-life heroes, Dr. Paul Rohlf, a urologist from Davenport, Iowa, recommended I receive treatment under the care of another real hero, Dr. John Donahue, and his urological team at the University of Indiana in Indianapolis, the same hospital where Lance Armstrong later would receive his treatment. After a complex surgery that left me an extensive abdominal incision with 33 staples, I left the hospital in early July a much different soon-to-be senior.

Even after all that, my main focus was recovering my strength and making it back so that I could play football as a senior. That was a little more than a month away. So my energies shifted to getting myself physically and mentally ready for competition. Surprisingly, my doctors reluctantly released me to participate and in early August with the support of my trainer, coaches, teammates, and family, I made it back to compete as a senior.

I felt a great sense of gratitude to get the chance to participate once again. They say it is impossible to be grateful and unhappy at the same time and I can attest to that. Although I trained to be a success, it was substantially more satisfying for me just to compete. Under the leadership of my head coaches — Gary Olson for football, Jeff Newmeister for wrestling, and Randy Denner for baseball — I competed once again, and they served as a great support system for me while I got back to doing what I loved. I have the greatest respect for those coaches and all their assistant coaches who did so much for me, a respect which certainly transcends athletics. Coach Denner held true to the promise he had made the year before and let me catch every doubleheader.

Today, I am lucky to say I am a cancer survivor. I am also lucky that I went through that experience as a young person. I have used that experience over the years in helping young people who are themselves trying to overcome adversity and facing some challenging times. Change is tough. It can sometimes take something significant like cancer to happen in our lives before we take a good hard look at ourselves and take the leap of faith to make the transformation that is needed. Occasionally, many of us may identify personal qualities that we would like to change about ourselves. Often we get into our routines and rarely take the opportunity to address those things and make the necessary changes. If nothing else, my cancer experience allowed me to realize how significant each and every day is. I've tried to use that concept in my teaching, coaching, and personal life. I work hard every day to try to make the most of my opportunities.

My all-time favorite movie is *It's a Wonderful Life*. I can watch that movie over and over and still have the same emotions when watching it as I did the very first time. The part of the movie that hits home with me is the idea that we have the chance to make such a significant impact on others while we make our way through life. The average teacher and coach like me does not receive the notoriety or prominence that more high-profile professionals do, but the ability to make a difference is still the same. I know most high-profile coaches would do the same thing without all the fame and publicity linked to their job. What you do matters, and in this job you will have an influence that stretches well beyond your sports involvement.

Work hard at building a winner but also work hard at being a champion for young people. Do things the right way and you will not regret for a second the time you have spent with all the lives you get a chance to touch. Coaching is an honorable profession, so be responsible and take pride in what you do. In the process, you will create for yourself great memories that will last a lifetime.

I cannot think of many things more special than being called "Coach." You have great opportunities ahead of you. Enjoy the ride and inspire greatness!

GAME DAY

Many people never heard of the name Tommy Gaul until the last couple of weeks in the sports section of newspapers. To me, Tommy Gaul represents the essence of what athletics is all about. His story is one that I experienced myself as an athlete. Tommy plays football for the University of Iowa Hawkeyes and I have gotten to know his parents during the last four years of traveling to games. They are two of the nicest people you could ever meet. We have had conversations on various topics over the years, but one that was much discussed was whether their son would ever get a chance to play in a game or just finish his career as a practice player. Playing Division I athletics is a fulltime job in terms of time commitment. Being a college student is tough enough, but when you add the sacrifices athletes make to play football, it becomes an even bigger challenge. Any coach will tell you that the importance of role players and scout team players is critical to team success. As a competitor, though, you are always aspiring to have a bigger role. Running out of the tunnel hand in hand in a swarm at Kinnick Stadium and wearing the Hawkeye uniform is a thrill, but at some point you want to get in the game, and contribute.

I attended the University of Iowa my first year as a student only. It did not take long for me to miss the game of football and take the leap of faith to transfer to Augustana College in Rock Island, Illinois, to continue to play the great game of football. I did not have the talent to be a Division I player. Augustana had established a tradition of excellence and I was not the type of player who was going to break the lineup immediately. So initially I filled a role as a practice/scout player and got my fix of football by preparing the starters for the games on Saturdays. When Augie would be crushing an opponent by 40 points, I would still be standing on the sidelines wondering how lopsided the score needed to be before I would get my chance to play. Frustrated as I was, I kept working.

With a consistent effort and positive attitude, the next season I was given a glimmer of hope as a special teams player and backup. At the end of crushing victories I might see a little cleanup action, but in my mind it was never significant playing time. I decided to keep on working. I was on track to graduate on time, so after missing football my freshman year at Iowa, my third year would be my final year playing football. I had never played more than a few series as a position player. Having spent most of the previous two years as a practice player, I felt the thought creep into my mind as to whether all of my efforts were really worth the sacrifice. Luckily, I had experienced what it was like to be a spectator at a game, and I knew I wanted to play *rather than watch. I had seen many more talented athletes quit over the years as they were not willing to accept a different role and were much too impatient waiting for their turn.*

Long story short, in my last year as a player, I trusted my coaches when they suggested I change positions, and I became a starter in all 12 games of our 1986 National Championship team. My commitment to football and patience as a player to do what I was told became life-changing for me. I found success in part because I was willing to trust the process and let my story play out.

Jenny and I attended the Hawkeye game on Saturday with some great friends, including former Saber Head Coach Dwight Spangler. Two plays into the first offensive series the guard was injured, and as the game went on I noticed the center had moved to guard and now playing at center was No. 57. Hoping I was correct, I scrambled to find the roster and I confirmed that No. 57 was Tommy Gaul. Tommy played the entire game and performed well against one of Indiana's talented defensive linemen.

Tommy was a fifth-year senior who was a walk-on from West Des Moines Dowling. In high school, he was a First Team All-State player and like all others, he had hopes and dreams of becoming a starter early in his career. What he was asked to do, though, was to trust the process and do what was asked of him. Over his five years, that is exactly what he did while many others in the program gave up and quit. Although he did not lose his drive to compete — and his lack of playing time caused a little anxiety in the family — he waited his turn and did everything that was asked of him. His time came on Saturday, two plays into the first series.

After the game, I told Jenny I wanted to stop by the players' entrance and talk to some parents. As much fun as the game was, talking with the Gauls and seeing how excited they were for their son's opportunity and performance was even better. In football, as in life, you never know when your moment is going to come. That is one of the reasons you keep working. You never quit.

"It is more likely that your *attitude*, rather than your *aptitude*, will determine your *altitude* in life?"

CHAPTER 9 ACTIVITIES

- Write a short note thanking a former coach in your life for being a positive influence in your life.

- Describe a time in your life where adversity served to make you a stronger person.

- Explain a time in your life when you quit something and what led up to you making that decision.

- Think of some ways you will bring balance to your life so that your sole focus is not the dynamics of athletics.

- What do you most enjoy about coaching and what do you most dislike about this profession?

ACKNOWLEDGMENTS

I want to thank my wife, Jenny, for supporting me in the pursuit of every goal and dream I've had through all the years. You are there to nudge me forward and be the voice of reason when I need it most. It has been amazing to watch you adapt to a life of sports even though you would have been perfectly happy without it. You are an incredible partner who always picked up the slack parenting while I was away coaching a team.

Thanks to my home team, Casey and Haley. I was always glad that you got to be a part of my journey in coaching. Growing up in a coaching family was unique for you because you had experiences only coaching families can relate to. How wonderful it was for me having you there every step of the way. You were great hosts to all the athletes, coaches, and teams I brought home from time to time. You always helped to remind me, though, that when it was family time, it was family time. Watching you compete created some of my favorite all-time memories and seeing you grow into the people we had dreamed you might become has been inspiring. Thank you, Casey and Haley, for letting me share some stories!

I am writing this in memory of my dad, Jack Kreiter, who helped direct me into education. I miss his guidance and conversations every day. Thanks to my mother, Myra, who continues to be our family's biggest cheerleader and has carried that tradition forward with each grandchild. To my sister, Tammy, you did not take the coaching route but we share the same core values and beliefs. A big shout-out to my brother, Eugene — it was always great to watch you coach your own team with the same passion and integrity. I relish the times we were able to coach together. I thank the Sbertoli family, too, for always being interested and supportive in what I was doing. I appreciate all the support from DeWitt, Grand Mound, Low Moor, and Welton, the communities that make up our school district of Central DeWitt.

Thank you, Mr. Howard Ehrler and Coach Dwight Spangler, for hiring this young naïve teacher-coach 30 years ago and giving me so many opportunities.

I can't say enough about all the loyal coaches I got a chance to work with over the years. Thanks for the commitments to our programs and athletes and your efforts in doing things the right way. Some of you stayed the course through all the good and the bad for a long time. Thanks to all my former coaches and mentors in coaching at all levels. You have all had an impact on my career and my life and showed me how to be a coach.

I am indebted to my editor, Christine Gilroy, whom I had the privilege of working alongside of as a colleague for many years. You have given me the confidence and encouragement to turn my thoughts into the words in this book. I would never have done it without you!

Last, I am appreciative of all the parents and especially the athletes I got to work with. It was a great pleasure to be part of your life for a while, and you provided me with memories that will last a lifetime. Thanks for all your efforts and great attitudes. I am proud of what you accomplished during our time together but even prouder of what you have done with your lives. I can't think of a bigger honor than to have been called "Coach" by you.

ABOUT THE AUTHOR

Kurt Kreiter is a graduate of North Scott High School, Eldridge, Iowa, where he was a three-sport athlete in football, wrestling, and baseball. He was inducted into their Athletic Hall of Fame in 1996. Active in drama, vocal music, and Fellowship of Christian Athletes, he was also Chapter president of FFA and president of 4-H Club. He was a member of the National Honor Society and president of his senior class.

Kurt attended the University of Iowa in Iowa City as a freshman but transferred to Augustana College in Rock, Island, Illinois, as a sophomore so he could continue to compete in athletics. He was a member of three national championship football teams at Augustana and was the starting defensive end for the 1986 team, which won the NCAA Division III National Championship at the Stagg Bowl in Phenix City, Ala. He ended his career on a team with seniors who won an unprecedented four national championships with a record of 49-0-1 during their four years. The 1986 defensive unit led the nation in defense, allowing opponents to just .83 yards per carry rushing. The 1984, 1985, and 1986 teams he was a part of have been inducted into *the Augustana Tribe of Vikings Hall of Fame.*

During his three-year collegiate athletic career, Kurt also wrestled. He was a two-time NCAA Division III National Championships qualifier and was an Academic All-American in 1987. He was a two-time individual conference champion on three conference champion teams for Augustana. He was the team captain.

After earning his bachelor of arts degree from Augustana in 1987, Kurt took a teaching and coaching position at Central Schools in DeWitt, Iowa, where he was a biology and Anatomy & Physiology teacher for 25 years. He earned his master of arts degree from Franciscan University, Clinton, Iowa, in 2005. He has been the district activities director since 2012.

For 25 years, Kurt coached football and wrestling at Central DeWitt as a middle school, assistant, and head coach. During his 20 years as head wrestling coach, he compiled a 213-173 career record, taking his 2007 team to a fourth-place finish at the IHSAA State Dual Tournament. In his 11 years as the head football coach of the Saber football team, he led the Saber program to the quarterfinals twice and into the post-season four times. For 12 years, Kurt competed as a member of the Quad Cities Irish Rugby Football Club.

Coach Kreiter is a 33-year testicular cancer survivor. He and his wife, Jenny, have been married for 29 years and have two children, Casey, 26, and Haley, 23. Both are graduates of the University of Iowa.

Casey graduated with a degree in science education. He played collegiate football for the Hawkeyes and earned All-Big Ten athletic and academic recognition and was named a permanent team captain of the 2013 team. He is currently the starting long snapper for the Denver Broncos. Casey and his wife, Meghan, were married in 2016. Haley completed her undergraduate degree in speech and hearing science, graduating with high distinction. She is currently a graduate student pursuing her master's degree in Speech-Language Pathology at the University of Iowa.

Order signed copies of

BECOME THE INSPIRATION

LEADERSHIP PRINCIPLES AND FUNDAMENTALS FOR THE BEGINNING COACH

To order multiple signed copies of this book for
coaching clinics, professional workshops,
and educational seminars, contact the author
at the following email account:

*1*coachkreiter@gmail.com

You are invited to use the same email
to ask Kurt Kreiter questions about coaching
or to leave comments about this book.
Please use the same email address or the book
listing at amazon.com to submit a review of

BECOME THE INSPIRATION

LONE OAK
BOOKS

Made in the USA
Lexington, KY
20 April 2017

Made in the USA
Middletown, DE
31 January 2017

After school the next day...

AT THE PARK..

Hi! WHAT HAPPENED WITH THE PRINCIPAL?

NOTHING REALLY. HE WAS JUST... UH... WELCOMING ME.

MR. WEBSTER IS PRETTY NICE. I GUESS. DENVER! WANNA PLAY?

WERE YOU WAITING TO PLAY?

GO AHEAD. THEY DON'T WANT ME ANYWAY.

HEY, GUYS, ALBERTO SHOULD GET TO PLAY. HE WAS HERE BEFORE I WAS.

WE ASKED YOU, MAN!

BESIDES, WE NEED ANOTHER PLAYER, NOT ANOTHER BASKETBALL!

HEY!

I DON'T WANT TO PLAY WITH PEOPLE WHO ACT LIKE THAT.

THANKS!

POW

SOMEBODY'S IN BIG TROUBLE NOW! YOU MESSED WITH THE WRONG GUY!

12

WHY DID HE PUSH ME DOWN?

SORRY! I DIDN'T MEAN TO DO THAT.

THE BALL KNOCKED THE CAN OVER. I WAS JUST TRYING TO CLEAN UP.

THANKS! YOU KNOW, WE DID A LOT OF CLEANING UP WHEN WE MOVED IN. THERE WERE BEER BOTTLES EVERYWHERE!

THAT DOESN'T EXPLAIN WHY HE KNOCKED ME DOWN! WHY WAS HE SO UPSET?

LET'S PLAY!

UH... OKAY.

THE NEXT DAY AFTER SCHOOL...

I HAVE TO TELL YOU WHAT HAPPENED YESTERDAY WITH DENVER, CHANTAL.

BZZ BZZZ BBZZ BZZ BZZZ!

THAT IS STRANGE!

SCHOOL BUS LINE

I CAN'T FIGURE OUT WHAT DENVER'S PROBLEM IS.

MAYBE WE SHOULD PRAY FOR HIM.

YEAH, GOD WILL HELP HIM.

HI, ALBERTO!

HI, SUKI!

WHAT'S THAT ABOUT?

I'LL TELL YOU ABOUT IT ON THE WAY TO YOUR HOUSE.

15

At school the next day...

Here goes nothing!

Suki, can we talk? Please?

Aren't you embarrassed to be seen with me?

Just listen!

Why should I?

So I can tell you how wrong I was!

You are going to admit that you were wrong? You?

If you ever give me a chance!

Go ahead.

I'm sorry I hurt you. I was worried about how people would react to my "different" sister.

I'm different, too!

I prayed about everything, and realized that I was so wrong! Like looks matter!

Yeah, so what if people make fun?

I never let it bother me when they thought my friends were strange!

Are you saying I'm strange?

No..I..I..I..

It's okay, Chantal. I get it.

Friends?

Friends!

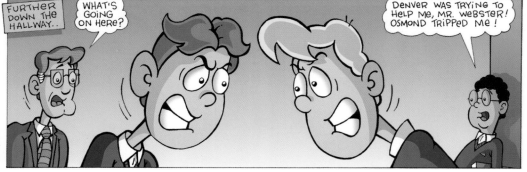

Further down the hallway..

What's going on here?

Denver was trying to help me, Mr. Webster! Osmond tripped me!

16

SORRY, PRINCIPAL WEBSTER!

THAT'S OKAY, DENVER. I'M GLAD YOU'RE BACK IN OUR SCHOOL.

THANKS.

WHAT ELSE CAN GO WRONG TODAY?

DOWN THE HALL...

LET'S FIND OUR FIRST CLASS.

I'M GOING TO LOOK FOR DENVER. I HAVEN'T SEEN HIM IN A COUPLE OF WEEKS.

I HAVE MS. POWER FOR HISTORY! YUCK!!

OKAY! SEE YOU LATER, ALBERTO!

BYE.

THERE'S DENVER NOW!

HI, DENVER!

CAN I BORROW SOME PAPER AND A PENCIL?

DON'T YOU HAVE ANY SUPPLIES???

I FORGOT, OKAY?

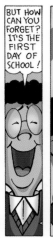

BUT HOW CAN YOU FORGET? IT'S THE FIRST DAY OF SCHOOL!

ARE YOU GOING TO LEND ME THE STUFF OR NOT, FATSO?!

HERE, YOU CAN USE THESE THINGS.

GET OUT OF THE WAY, SHAMU.

I WISH IT WAS ALREADY THE LAST DAY OF SCHOOL!

19

Two weeks later at Chantal's house...

WWWAAAAAAAAAAAAAAAAAA!!

OH NO! NOT AGAIN! THAT BABY CRIES ALL THE TIME!!

WHAT'S SHE CRYING ABOUT NOW?

MAYBE SHE'S HUNGRY.

MAYBE SHE'S FEELING LONELY.

ALL ABOUT BABIES

MAYBE SHE'S A PAIN!

CHANTAL! DON'T TALK THAT WAY ABOUT YOUR SISTER!

BUT HOW AM I SUPPOSED TO GET ANY SLEEP?

I'LL GET HER BOTTLE.

IT'S OKAY, AMANDA. DON'T CRY, SWEETIE.

THINGS SURE HAVE CHANGED AROUND HERE!

WWWAAAAAAAAAAAAAAAAAAAA!!

THE NEXT MORNING AT SCHOOL...

I CAN'T WAIT TO TALK TO CHANTAL!

I HAVE TO TALK TO ALBERTO!

HEY, CHANTAL! I LIKE YOUR HAIR LIKE THAT! HOW ARE THINGS WITH THE BABY?

DON'T ASK!

UM...ALBERTO, CAN WE TALK?

I DON'T THINK SO! I'VE GOT TO GO.

20

21

23

Next day...

24

Later at home...

26

PRINCIPAL WEBSTER'S OFFICE...

DENVER, YOU'VE BEEN DOING SO WELL THIS YEAR. IS SOMETHING WRONG?

NO.

IS THERE ANY WAY THAT I CAN HELP YOU?

NO.

OKAY THEN. I'M ASSIGNING YOU SATURDAY DETENTION. I'LL CALL YOUR MOTHER LATER TODAY

WHATEVER.

AFTER SCHOOL AT DENVER'S HOUSE..

HI, DENVER! HERE'S THE WORKSHEET WE DID WHILE YOU WERE GONE FROM MATH CLASS TODAY.

OH, YEAH .. UH .. THANKS.

DENVER! GET IN HERE!

SEE YOU TOMORROW!

WHATEVER.

I WONDER WHAT HE WAS DOING IN THAT FLOWER POT.

SLAM

OH NO! ALBERTO WAS RIGHT!

BEER BEER

At school the next day...

OH.. UM.. HI, DENVER!

YEAH, GOOD MORNING, DENVER!

HOW'S IT GOING, DENVER?

HE DIDN'T SAY A WORD TO US!

HE LOOKS LIKE HE'S ALREADY BEEN DRINKING THIS MORNING!

WE HAVE TO GET HIM SOME HELP!

BUT IF WE TELL, HE'LL GET IN TROUBLE!

WE'RE HIS FRIENDS. WE HAVE TO...

OH NO! THE BELL! LATE AGAIN!

LATER AT LUNCH...

YOU DON'T NEED THIS, FAT BOY.

HEY!

HEY, ALBERTO, DON'T LET PEOPLE LIKE OSMOND GET YOU DOWN. YOU'RE A GREAT PERSON!

THANKS, SUKI.

I DON'T THINK YOU REALIZE HOW GREAT YOU ARE, SUKI.

OH, SURE! EVERYBODY JUST LOVES ME!

YOU KNOW, ALBERTO, EVERYTHING HAS CHANGED WITH CHANTAL. SHE NEVER HAS TIME FOR ME ANYMORE.

MY MATH NOTEBOOK

SHE'S STILL YOUR FRIEND, SUKI! SHE'S JUST BUSY WITH THE BABY--THAT'S ALL!

I...GUESS, ALBERTO.

28

AFTER SCHOOL AT DENVER'S HOUSE...

HI, DENVER!

ALBERTO, SUKI AND I WOULD REALLY LIKE TO HELP YOU WITH YOUR PROBLEM.

I DON'T NEED YOUR HELP!

IF YOU DON'T WANT OUR HELP, YOU SHOULD PRAY AND ASK GOD TO HELP YOU.

YEAH, RIGHT! PRAYING DOESN'T WORK!

IT DOES, TOO!

WHATEVER. I HAVE TO GO IN NOW.

I'LL PRAY FOR YOU, DENVER. AND SO WILL SUKI AND ALBERTO.

GO AHEAD AND PRAY, CHANTAL, ...

IF IT MAKES YOU FEEL BETTER. BUT..

STAY OUT OF MY LIFE!!

29

At Chantal's house the next day...

DENVER, YOU CAN STAY HERE ALL DAY IF NECESSARY.

LATER AT SUKI'S...

CHANTAL ISN'T AT HOME! AGAIN! I'M NOT GOING TO LEAVE A MESSAGE THIS TIME. SHE NEVER CALLS BACK!

HEY, BIG SISTER! WANT TO PLAY WITH US?

I GUESS. IT'S NOT LIKE I HAVE ANY FRIENDS, DO I?

ON THE WAY TO DENVER'S HOUSE..

I'M GLAD YOU FINISHED YOUR WORK, DENVER. EVEN IF IT DID TAKE A LITTLE LONGER!

YES, SIR.

THANKS FOR WALKING ME HOME, PRINCIPAL WEBSTER.

I'LL SEE YOU.

YOU.. DON'T HAVE TO COME IN OR ANYTHING.

BYE.

COULD YOU INTRODUCE ME TO YOUR MOTHER? I'D LIKE TO TALK TO HER.

YES, SIR.

PLEASE, GOD, DON'T LET MOM EMBARRASS ME!

31

A few days later...

I DON'T DRINK, SUKI! IT'S MY MOM, OKAY?

IT'S TRUE, SUKI.

YOU KNEW?

YES, BUT I FELT IT WAS DENVER'S DECISION WHETHER TO TELL YOU OR NOT.

IS YOUR MOM GETTING HELP, DENVER?

YES!

SHE WAS ORDERED TO GO TO REHAB BECAUSE OF DRUNK DRIVING.

THERE'S THE BELL. YOU'D BETTER GET TO CLASS NOW.

YES, SIR.

OKAY.

OUT IN THE HALL...

I KNOW YOU WERE TRYING TO HELP, SUKI. THANKS!

WHATEVER.

LATER IN CHANTAL'S CLASS...

CLASS, YOU HAVE FIVE MINUTES LEFT TO FINISH THE TEST!

YOU CAN GO TO THE OFFICE RIGHT NOW, CHANTAL!!

I WILL NOT TOLERATE CHEATING!!

Later at home...

34

35

The next evening...

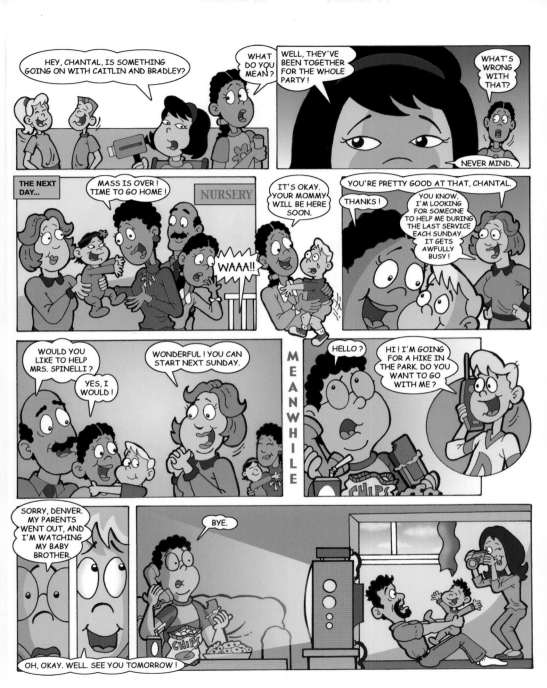

39

The next day at school...

LOOK! MIA IS SITTING WITH DAVID.

M-HM.

EVERYONE'S GETTING A BOYFRIEND!

THAT'S NOT TRUE, SUKI.

IT'S JUST A FEW PEOPLE. AND ANYWAY--IT'S NOT LIKE THEY'RE DATING OR ANYTHING.

I GUESS.

I WONDER IF A BOY WILL EVER LIKE ME - A GIRL IN A WHEELCHAIR?

DID YOU LEAVE ANY FOOD FOR THE REST OF US?

HEY, SUKI, ARE YOU GOING TO EAT THAT COOKIE?

NO, YOU CAN HAVE IT.

HI, DENVER! HOW ARE THINGS AT HOME?

GREAT! JUST GREAT!

THANKS!

GLAD TO HEAR IT. SEE YOU LATER!

bye.

40

41

That weekend...

42

LATER IN THE HALL...

HAVE YOU GUYS WORKED ON YOUR FAMILY HISTORY PROJECT?

I'M WRITING DOWN QUESTIONS FOR THE INTERVIEW WITH MY GRANDPARENTS.

MY PARENTS ARE HELPING ME WITH MY FAMILY TREE.

HOW ABOUT YOU, DENVER?

WAIT UNTIL YOU SEE MY SCRAPBOOK!

I'LL GET AROUND TO IT. WHAT'S THE BIG HURRY?

THERE'S NO RUSH, I GUESS, BUT...OH... HI, YAZID.

UH...HI, ALBERTO!

LOOK, DON'T WORRY ABOUT ME. I'LL GET THE STUPID PROJECT DONE, OKAY?

SURE, DENVER.

OKAY.

NO PROBLEM.

AFTER SCHOOL...

DING

DONG

WHY DOESN'T ANYONE ANSWER THE DOOR? WHERE'S ALBERTO?

OH, WELL. I GUESS NO ONE IS HOME.

Meanwhile at Suki's house...

44

45

THE NEXT DAY IN THE SCHOOL CAFETERIA...

47

At school the next day...

48

49

I JUST WANTED TO TELL YOU THAT YOU'RE DOING A FANTASTIC JOB, CHANTAL.

I AM?

YOU SURE ARE! YOU HAVE A REAL KNACK FOR WORKING WITH KIDS. I THINK YOU WOULD MAKE A GREAT TEACHER.

TEACHER OF THE YEAR

THANKS, MRS. SPINELLI.

WOULD YOU LIKE TO HELP ME WITH THE DAY CAMP THIS SUMMER?

SIGN UP FOR SUMMER CAMP

I...I...I...

THINK ABOUT IT, OKAY?

YES, MA'AM. SEE YOU NEXT WEEK!

HEY, GUESS WHAT, YOU GUYS?

A FEW DAYS LATER, THE KIDS GO ON A FIELD TRIP TO THE MUSEUM.   SUKI CAPTURES IT ALL ON VIDEO...

MUSEUM ENTRANCE

HI, SUKI!

LOOK! AN APPLE FOR THE TEACHER!

FRUIT

THIS GUY HAS NOTHING ON ME!

TARZAN

SAY SOMETHING, YAZID!

EH... I...

WHAT'S THE MATTER WITH YAZID?

YOU WON'T BELIEVE IT, BUT ...BUZZ...BUZZ... BUZZ...BUZZ..

WOW! HE DOES?

HEY, DENVER! SMILE FOR THE CAMERA!

JUST LEAVE ME ALONE, SUKI. I DON'T FEEL LIKE GOOFING AROUND.

VOLCA

OKAY. SORRY!

LATER..

THAT WAS A GOOD GAME!

YEAH.

THANKS FOR ALL YOUR HELP, DENVER. EXERCISING WITH YOU HAS MADE ME FEEL A LOT BETTER.

PROMISE ME THAT YOU'LL KEEP ON EXERCISING, ALBERTO, NO MATTER WHAT.

YOU BET I WILL!

SO DO YOU PROMISE?

OKAY! I PROMISE. I HAVE TO GO IN NOW. SEE YOU LATER!

GOOD BYE, ALBERTO.

IT'S BEEN NICE KNOWING YOU.

The next day...

LISTEN... I.. UH.. WELL... YOU HAVE THIS... FRIEND ...AND..

I KNOW WHO YOU MEAN. SHE'S REALLY NICE. WHY DON'T YOU TALK TO HER?

MAYBE I WILL SOMETIME!

AFTER SCHOOL...

HEY, YOU GUYS! I HAVE AN IDEA ABOUT DENVER!

YOU DO?

SCHOOL BUS LINE

LISTEN! HIS MOM SIGNED HIM OUT, BUT MAYBE THEY HAVEN'T ACTUALLY MOVED YET.

LET'S SEE IF THEY'RE STILL THERE!

VERY SOON...

DING DONG

THERE'S A CAR IN THE DRIVEWAY SO SOMEONE IS HERE!

HI. IS DENVER HERE?

NO. THE JACKSONS MOVED.

SLAM

NO.

A week later...

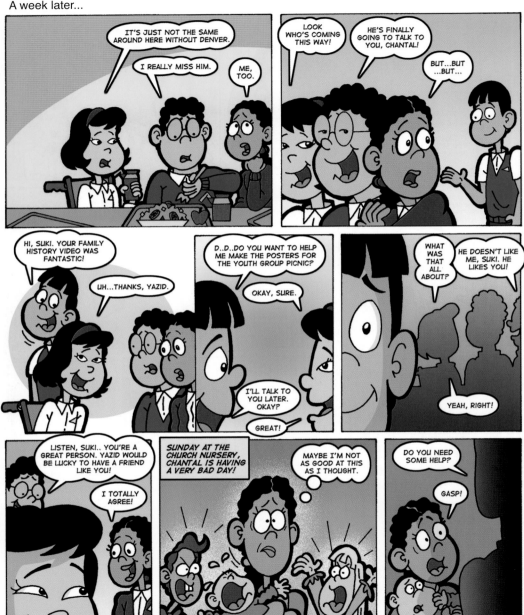

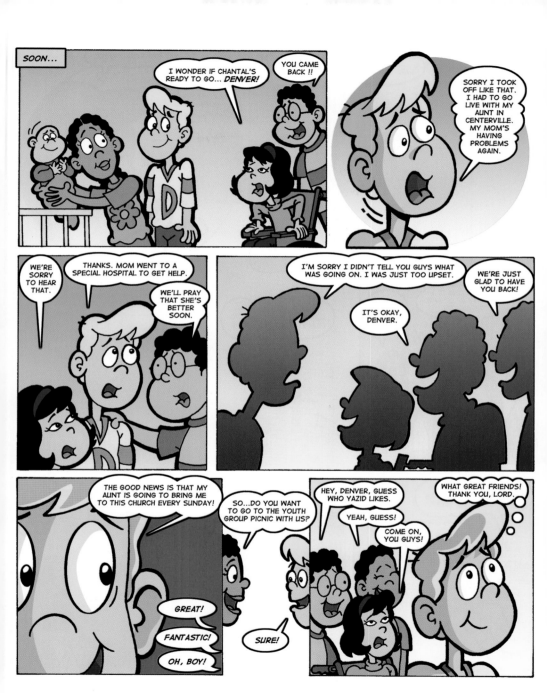

55

STEPPING STONES

The Fourth Collection

...AND I'M GOING TO WORK REALLY HARD THIS YEAR AND GET GOOD GRADES.

REC 7:32 AM

THAT WAS GREAT, YAZID!

I CAN'T WAIT TO SEE YOUR MOVIE, SUKI.

I'M CALLING IT *FIRST DAY OF SCHOOL: THE MOVIE!*

SOUNDS GREAT! SEE YOU LATER!

THERE'S CHANTAL AND ALBERTO'S BUS! I HAVE TO FILM THEM FOR MY MOVIE.

WOW, ALBERTO! ALL THAT EXERCISE AND HEALTHY EATING HAVE REALLY PAID OFF! YOU LOOK GREAT!

AND I FEEL GREAT, TOO.

REC 7:3_ _M

SAY SOMETHING FOR MY MOVIE, ALBERTO. WHAT ARE YOUR PLANS THIS YEAR?

TO LEARN A LOT AND HAVE FUN!

HI, CHANTAL!

HHHMMM... WHATEVER.

HI!

WHAT'S THE MATTER, CHANTAL?

I'M SO TIRED. AMANDA WAS SICK ALL NIGHT, AND I DIDN'T GET MUCH SLEEP.

HI, DENVER!

YOU'RE BACK!!

HI!

YES, I AM BACK. MOM JUST ENROLLED ME.

AND GUESS WHAT? MOM IS OUT OF REHAB AND DOING GREAT!

FANTASTIC!

THAT'S GOOD NEWS!

DO YOU WANT TO BE IN MY MOVIE ABOUT THE FIRST DAY OF SCHOOL?

OKAY!

THIS YEAR WILL BE GREAT BECAUSE I'M BACK WITH MY FRIENDS.

REC
7:32 AM

THERE'S THE BELL. SEE YOU GUYS LATER.

WE'D BETTER GET TO P.E.

HEY, YOU'RE REALLY LOOKING GOOD, ALBERTO!

AFTER SCHOOL...

MOM! DENVER'S BACK IN OUR SCHOOL!

THAT'S NICE. LET'S WASH YOUR HAIR, AMANDA.

SHE'S ALWAYS BUSY WITH AMANDA.

I SHOULDN'T BE SO IMMATURE. AMANDA'S BEEN SICK A LOT LATELY.

I'LL GO START SUPPER, MOM.

MEANWHILE...

I GOT SOME REALLY GOOD VIDEO TODAY. IF I JUST ...WAIT A MINUTE! WHAT'S THAT IN THE BACKGROUND?

I'LL JUST REWIND...THERE! WHAT ARE THEY DOING? IT LOOKS LIKE...

REW

OH, IT'S PROBABLY NOTHING. NOTHING AT ALL!

LATER AT THE PARK..

YOU WON'T BELIEVE WHAT I HEARD!

WHAT?

TY RK

LECH TOLD ME OSMOND'S PARENTS HAD A HUGE FIGHT! EVERYONE ON THE BLOCK COULD HEAR THEM YELLING!

THAT'S TOO BAD.

OSMOND'S DAD LEFT. LECH THINKS THEY'RE BREAKING UP.

OH, NO!

I FEEL SORRY FOR OSMOND.

ME, TOO.

At youth group...

LET ME GET A SHOT OF THOSE LEAVES.

SUKI! YOU'RE IN MY WAY! DO YOU ALWAYS HAVE TO VIDEOTAPE EVERYTHING?

EVERYBODY LIKED *FIRST DAY OF SCHOOL –THE MOVIE!* THEY'LL LOVE MY YOUTH GROUP MOVIE.

BUT YOU'RE DRIVING ME NUTS WITH THAT CAMERA!

JUST WAIT UNTIL SHE'S A WORLD-FAMOUS DIRECTOR, CHANTAL.

YEAH, CHANTAL. I'LL MAKE YOU A STAR.

I'M READY FOR MY CLOSEUP!

LATER! I NEED TO FILM THE KIDS DECORATING THE BAKE SALE COOKIES.

THE NEXT DAY AT SCHOOL...

YOU'RE KIDDING! SHE DID?

AMANDA WAS SICK AGAIN LAST NIGHT. I HOPE SHE'S..

HEY, GUESS WHAT I HEARD?

60

62

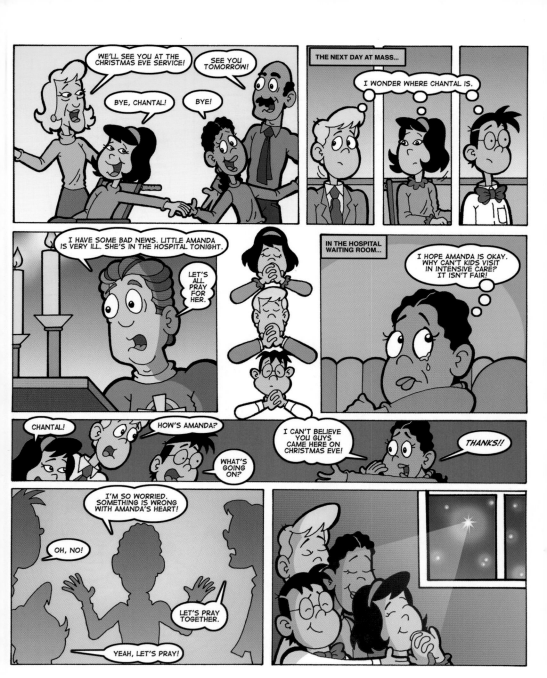

At school the next day...

Next day at school...

66

The next morning...

WOW! THERE ARE A LOT OF PEOPLE FROM CHURCH HERE!

WAITING ROOM

BUT WHERE ARE CHANTAL AND HER PARENTS?

HI, KIDS! CHANTAL WILL BE SO GLAD TO HAVE HER FRIENDS HERE!

WHERE IS SHE, FATHER?

THE DOCTOR GAVE HER PERMISSION TO VISIT HER SISTER BEFORE THE SURGERY. THE WHOLE FAMILY IS TOGETHER RIGHT NOW.

I HOPE EVERYTHING WILL BE OKAY

LET'S WAIT OVER THERE.

OKAY.

IN THE ICU....

I'M WORRIED ABOUT THIS OPERATION.

WE ARE, TOO, HONEY, BUT GOD IS WITH US.

IT'S ALL IN *HIS* HANDS.

CHANTAL...WE...WE'RE SORRY ABOUT ...THE WAY WE'VE BEEN ARGUING.

I'VE BEEN AFRAID THAT YOU MIGHT SPLIT UP.

OH, HONEY! WE DIDN'T MEAN TO SCARE YOU LIKE THAT!

The next day...

OOPS! I FORGOT MY MATH BOOK.

DID YOU SEE THAT HUMONGOUS BELT BUCKLE? *ELVIS LIVES!*

YEAH! WHAT CRAZY THING WILL HE WEAR NEXT?

THAT NIGHT AT SUKI'S...

WE'RE ALMOST READY FOR DINNER. COULD YOU GET THE BOYS, SUKI?

YES, GRANDMA.

LEE! JUSTIN! WHERE ARE THEY? HEY, WHAT'S THAT?

IT'S GRANDPA'S PILL BOTTLE. WHY IS THIS IN THE BOY'S ROOM?

OH NO! WHERE ARE THE PILLS? DID THE BOYS TAKE THEM?

71

YAZID, I FINALLY FIGURED OUT WHEN YOU SHOULD TELL ON SOMEBODY.

WHEN?

IF SOMEONE COULD GET HURT, YOU HAVE TO TELL. SO I TALKED TO MY GRANDPARENTS ABOUT THE PILLS.

THEY AGREED WITH ME THAT I SHOULD TELL FATHER DAVID AND PRINCIPAL WEBSTER.

YOU DID THE RIGHT THING. NOW THAT PERSON CAN GET HELP. WHO WAS IT ANYWAY?

I'M NOT TELLING! I DON'T GOSSIP...REMEMBER?

WHAT'S THE MATTER, ALBERTO?

I HEARD SUKI AND CHANTAL TALKING YESTERDAY.

THEY THINK MY NEW STYLES LOOK STUPID.

SEE YOU LATER, DENVER.

WOW! IT REALLY CAN HURT WHEN PEOPLE TALK ABOUT YOU!!

LATER AT CHANTAL'S HOUSE

IT'S SO NICE TO HAVE THE WHOLE FAMILY AT HOME!

I WAS GETTING TIRED OF THE HOSPITAL.

TIME FOR AMANDA'S MEDICATION.

GET WELL

THINKING OF YOU!

EVERYONE HAS BEEN SO KIND TO US.

HOW CAN WE THANK ALL OF THEM?

AMANDA'S NOT BREATHING WELL!

WE HAVE TO GET HER TO THE HOSPITAL!!

The following day...

STEPPING STONES

The Fifth Collection

77

But the next day...

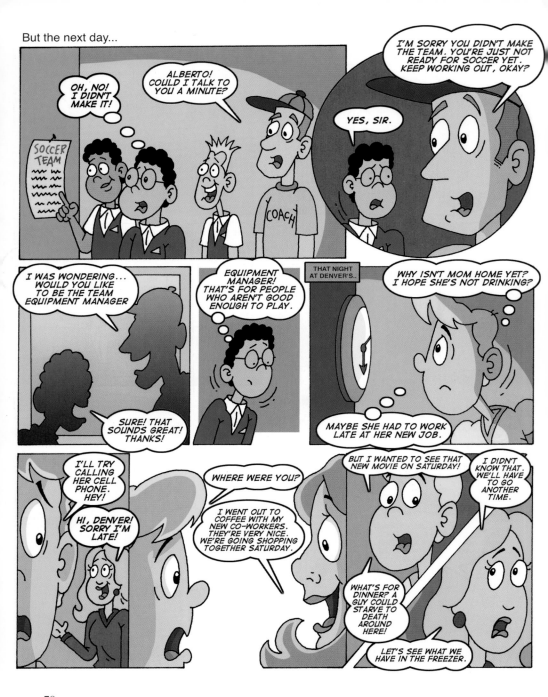

THE NEXT DAY AT SCHOOL...

HI, SUKI.

COULD WE BE IN YOUR NEXT VIDEO, SUKI?

SURE!

HEY, MAYBE I COULD SHOOT THE VIDEO AT THE MALL!

THAT'S A GREAT IDEA!

UH... SUKI?

HI, CHANTAL! HOW'S YOUR LITTLE SISTER DOING?

SHE'S FEELING OKAY THESE DAYS BUT SOMETIMES SHE...

I KNOW! YOU COULD ALL BE SHOWING THE LATEST FASHIONS!

GREAT!

SUKI NEVER HAS TIME FOR ME ANYMORE.

MAYBE YOU SHOULD TALK TO HER ABOUT THAT AT YOUTH GROUP TONIGHT.

GOOD IDEA!

THAT NIGHT AT YOUTH GROUP...

I CAN'T BELIEVE SHE'S NOT HERE!

HI, CHANTAL! WHERE'S SUKI?

I DON'T KNOW AND I DON'T CARE!

WE'RE NOT FRIENDS ANYMORE!

79

Weeks later...

81

A few weeks go by...

...AND WE'RE GOING TO HAVE HOT COCOA AT THE PARTY.

IT SOUNDS GREAT. THANKS FOR INVITING ME.

SUKI AND ALBERTO ARE INVITED, TOO. SEE YOU LATER!

BYE!

FINALLY I'LL GET TO DO SOMETHING WITH SUKI!!

HEY, CHANTAL, I NEED YOUR OPINION ON WHAT I SHOULD GET SUKI FOR CHRISTMAS.

OKAY.

WHICH DO YOU THINK SHE'D LIKE BETTER?

WELL..UM.. THE SCARF!

THANKS FOR YOUR HELP!

SURE!

THOSE ARE EXPENSIVE GIFTS! I'LL HAVE TO GET SUKI SOMETHING REALLY GOOD FOR CHRISTMAS!

LATER..

SWISH

THAT'S IT FOR TODAY! EVERYONE HIT THE SHOWERS!

THE TEAM IS LOOKING BETTER THIS YEAR.

NO THANKS TO ME!

YOUR HELP IS IMPORTANT, ALBERTO!

THANKS, SUKI.

EQUIPMEN

COACH

YEAH, RIGHT!

82

A few days later...

At school the next day...

86

In the cafeteria the next day...

The following day...

90

91

Later...

At school the next day...

SATURDAY

95

97

The next day at school...

A COUPLE OF DAYS LATER, DENVER AND YAZID GET A TOUR OF THE SHELTER WITH THE OTHER VOLUNTEERS..

WE'VE FIXED UP SOME OF OUR CHURCH CLASSROOMS. HOMELESS FAMILIES CAN STAY HERE UNTIL THEY GET BACK ON THEIR FEET.

WE HAVE ADULT VOLUNTEERS TO HELP THE FAMILIES WITH THINGS LIKE EDUCATION, JOBS, AND HOUSING.

THIS IS GREAT, MR. PATRICK!

YOU YOUNG VOLUNTEERS CAN HELP COOK, CLEAN UP, AND PLAY WITH THE CHILDREN STAYING HERE. WE REALLY APPRECIATE YOUR HELP!

SEE YOU LATER. THANKS AGAIN!

THIS IS GOING TO BE A GOOD PROJECT.

I CAN'T WAIT TO GET STARTED.

AT THE HOSPITAL..

I THINK I'VE EXPLAINED EVERYTHING, BUT FEEL FREE TO ASK QUESTIONS AT ANY TIME.

OKAY, THANKS, MRS. MOREAU.

HEY, COULD I READ A STORY TO THE KIDS?

THAT WOULD BE GREAT!

WHAT ARE YOU DOING HERE?

101

Merry Christmas!

103

After Christmas vacation...

THE SHELTER KITCHEN...

HI, GEORGE!

HEY. HOW ABOUT HELPING ME TAKE OUT THIS TRASH?

OKAY.

NOW WE CAN TAKE A BREAK. WANT ONE?

THANKS! I'VE BEEN DYING FOR A SMOKE ALL DAY.

THE HOSPITAL PLAY ROOM...

"SO THEN THE LITTLE MOUSE SAID..."

HI, EVERYBODY!

I WASN'T FINISHED WITH MY STORY, MADISON.

WOW!

BALLOONS!

TOO BAD! THE KIDS LIKE THE BALLOONS BETTER.

THEY WERE ENJOYING MY STORY UNTIL YOU INTERRUPTED!

OKAY, EVERYBODY! COME AND CHOOSE A BALLOON!

THE NURSING HOME...

BUT. YOU. NEED. TO. EAT. IT'S. GOOD. FOR. YOU.

I ALREADY ATE! I TOLD YOU THAT THREE TIMES!

WHAT ARE YOU DOING, SUKI? THAT TRAY GOES TO ROOM 205.

OH! I THOUGHT YOU SAID ROOM 209. I'M SORRY!

I DON'T WANT THAT GIRL HELPING ME. I LIKE THAT NICE ALBERTO.

OKAY, MRS. RILEY.

THE NEXT MORNING...

HI, YOU GUYS! WHAT ARE YOU TALKING ABOUT?

OUR SERVICE PROJECTS!

HELPING OUT AT THE NURSING HOME IS GREAT! ISN'T IT, SUKI?

SURE. GREAT.

I WISH THINGS WERE LIKE THAT AT THE HOSPITAL. I'M HAVING A PROBLEM WITH...

WHAT'S THAT SMELL?

I SMELL IT, TOO.

WHAT IS THAT?

IT'S COMING FROM YOU, DENVER.

IT SMELLS LIKE...OH, NO!

HAVE YOU BEEN SMOKING, DENVER?

I...UH...I.....

105

107

At school the next day...

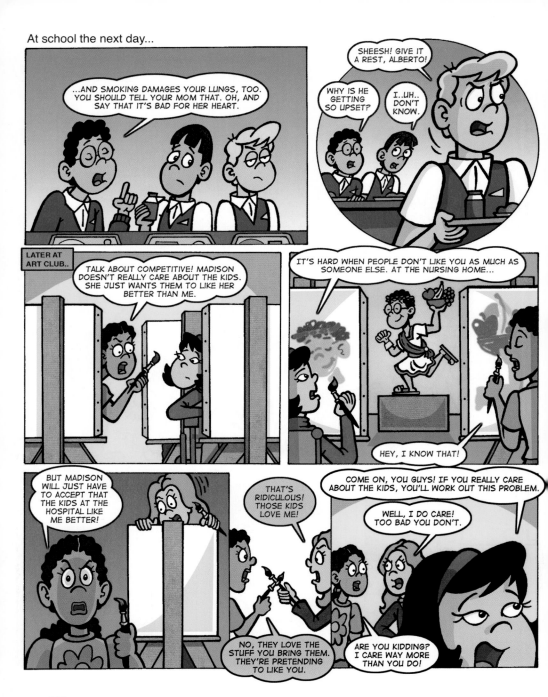

At Denver's house...

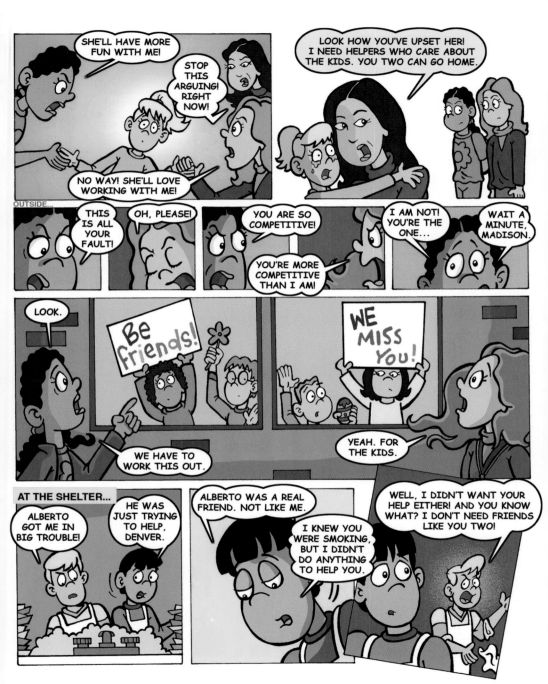

111

113

Next Day at School...

HI. CAN I...UM..EAT LUNCH WITH YOU GUYS?

I GUESS.

OKAY.

I'M REALLY SORRY ABOUT EVERYTHING. I KNOW YOU GUYS WERE ACTING LIKE TRUE FRIENDS. AND,,,AND I WASN'T. SORRY!

IT'S OKAY, DENVER.

YEAH!

I'M SO GLAD EVERYTHING IS COOL BETWEEN US. THANKS!

Alberto

Some old sayings are really true. Like "A friend in need is a friend indeed." And "Better late than never." (That's a good one for me!) One of my favorite sayings is, "Try, try again." It's hard to follow, but it's made a big difference in my life!

When people used to pick on me because of my weight, I wanted to say mean stuff back. I even thought about punching a few guys! But I knew it wasn't right to treat others that way so I didn't let myself strike back. It was a struggle to do that again and again, let me tell you! But prayer gave me the strength to keep trying. And knowing I had friends on my side helped, too.

Friends also helped when I felt like giving up on good nutrition and exercise. Everybody really encouraged me to keep going—especially Denver! He showed me that hard stuff is easier with a friend beside you. And you can reach a tough goal little by little if you just stick to it!

Of course, it's discouraging to keep trying and not get what you want. I thought about giving up on sports so many times. But when I made the baseball team, I was so glad I didn't quit. And I finally realized it had done me some good to keep trying. Like I learned I could handle let-downs. And I found out that people appreciated how they could depend on me.

I wish that trying hard could <u>make</u> things go my way, but life just doesn't work like that. Still, I know if I just keep trying, I'll get something out of my efforts. Even if I don't accomplish exactly what I wanted, I've learned it's worth it to try, try again!

Chantal

Alberto's right that you can't make things happen just how you want. I know that! But I still like the idea of controlling my life. I wish everything could be perfect—including me! Sometimes my control issues have caused trouble, but I've been working on that problem.

It used to be I couldn't accept being wrong about anything. I tried to cover up mistakes and make excuses. And I had a hard time apologizing because I had to admit I wasn't right about something. Now I realize there are more important things than looking perfect! Like owning up when you mess up—and caring about other people's feelings enough to say you're sorry.

And I think I finally get it that I can't control other people. When I work with kids in the church nursery or at the hospital, I want them to do exactly what I say when I say to do it. But kids are people—not robots! I can teach and encourage them, but I have to let them have their own minds. That goes for my friends, too. I shouldn't have tried to keep Suki from having other friends. People change. It isn't right to make them stay the same for you!

Hey, it's not like life stays the same either! Things are always changing. When Amanda became part of our family, she caused problems, disrupted our routines, and turned our lives upside down. She also made us all love her to pieces! How could I have controlled any of that? And her illness? That was like a runaway roller coaster! But with God's help, my family got through it all.

That's the most important thing I've learned about control. God's the one who has it. If I trust him, I can handle anything!

Denver

People always say life isn't easy. Hey, don't I know it! I've had some pretty tough times. Sometimes I made my problems worse by how I acted. But I've also learned how to handle things better.

Like I used to let my temper control me. I got into a lot of fights—with words and fists, too. I made excuses about why that was okay. The other guy pushed my buttons! I was defending a friend! But really I was mad about my problems—especially my mom's issues with drinking. Hiding my troubles and holding in my feelings made me a human volcano!

Then I met some friends who supported me even when I took my anger out on them. I finally learned it's okay to share your problems with friends and let them help you. That's what they're there for!

I also realized there are adults who want to help. Principal Webster took a real interest in me and found me a great counseling program. Teachers and coaches cared about me—and so did the adults involved in youth group and my service project. And, of course, Mom always loved me!

I used to act like it was me against the whole world. Finally I realized I'm not alone. I have so many caring people in my life. And, best of all, God is always there for me. Always!

Dealing with my issues has changed my life. Not that I'm perfect! Sometimes I'm not the friend I should be. And I still make some bad decisions. (Why did I think smoking would make me cool? Duh!) But I'm doing a better job of controlling my emotions instead of letting them control me.

Yeah, life isn't easy. But now I feel like I can deal with it!

Suki

I agree with Denver that friends are so important. I don't know what I'd do without my friends! But I have to admit that sometimes I've looked at friendship in a selfish way. I acted like it was all about me!

For example, I used to be too sensitive. I thought people were noticing things about me that they didn't like. Of course, not everybody feels comfortable with someone in a wheelchair. And there are people who are prejudiced against other races. But I was always worrying that people might find something wrong with me. When I was feeling insecure like that, I expected my friends to focus on me and tiptoe around my feelings. Like when Chantal was concerned about getting a sister from China, I took her attitude personally.

And I hate to say it, but there were other times when I treated friendship like a one-way street. I thought friends should pay plenty of attention to me— even when I wasn't paying attention to the problems in their lives! And if a friend let me down, I had a hard time forgiving. But, of course, I expected everybody to excuse my mistakes!

Now I get that a real friend doesn't just take, take, take! A real friend cares about the other person—and gives from the heart.

Yeah, I've learned a lot about true friendship. I used to think having a boyfriend was more important than having a friend. And I really made some mistakes when I got into the whole popularity thing. Hey, sometimes I still mess things up with my friends! I'm just so glad that God blessed me with each one of them. And I'm going to work hard at being the kind of friend they'll want to keep forever!

St. Paul
School News

Back to Sc

Welcome bac
Paul Catho
for anothe
school y
though
and v
doe
S

From the Office of
Principal Webster

Dear Parents and Teachers,

Kids face tough challenges today! Besides the normal difficulties of growing up, many deal with serious problems like peer pressure, substance abuse, and family dysfunction. Talking to kids about the issues in their lives can be difficult—I know! Here are some suggestions for communicating with the children you care about:

- **Share the media.** Check out the television programs, movies, books, and Web sites kids like, and use them to spark discussion. Talking casually about a character who smokes or drinks can be more effective than endless lectures. Sensitive questions become easier to ask and to answer when they're about a fictional situation.

- **Don't just talk.** Chat with kids while doing something else. Kids feel safer about opening up when you're not having an "official" talk. And if things get uncomfortable, you don't even have to look at each other! Parents can try this when traveling in the car or sharing chores. Teachers might give it a go when kids are drawing or coloring.

• **Listen!** Give kids plenty of time to express their feelings. When you jump in with judgments and opinions, they don't feel respected. Use encouraging sounds ("uh-huh") or expressions ("Really?") to keep things going, and then be quiet.

• **Lead gently.** Once the whole story's out and you start talking, avoid criticism. Instead, guide kids in self-examination with specific questions like "How did that work out?" or "What will you do next time?" Gently lead them to their own solutions whenever possible and help them plan for the future.

• **Assure kids they're not alone.** Tell them you care and you want to help. Welcome them to turn to you at any time. Pray for them—and with them. And, most importantly, remind kids that God loves them—and he's always there.

Sincerely,
Principal Webster

Did you enjoy spending time with the *Stepping Stones* kids?

If you did, you may want to read another comic collection by Diana R. Jenkins. Here's a sneak preview of what it's all about!

Once upon a time,
  there were a brother and sister named Paul and Cecilia.

Paul and Cecilia found some amazing old things in their attic…

…including an old flute and some mysterious sheet music!

When Cecilia played the music…

…the two ended up in a place they'd never seen before!

Saints of Note: The Comic Collection
Available from Pauline Books & Media in August 2009!

BOOKS & MEDIA

The Daughters of St. Paul operate book and media centers at the following addresses. Visit, call or write the one nearest you today, or find us on the World Wide Web, www.pauline.org

CALIFORNIA
3908 Sepulveda Blvd, Culver City, CA 90230 — 310-397-8676
2640 Broadway Street, Redwood City, CA 94063 — 650-369-4230
5945 Balboa Avenue, San Diego, CA 92111 — 858-565-9181

FLORIDA
145 S.W. 107th Avenue, Miami, FL 33174 — 305-559-6715

HAWAII
1143 Bishop Street, Honolulu, HI 96813 — 808-521-2731
Neighbor Islands call: — 866-521-2731

ILLINOIS
172 North Michigan Avenue, Chicago, IL 60601 — 312-346-4228

LOUISIANA
4403 Veterans Memorial Blvd, Metairie, LA 70006 — 504-887-7631

MASSACHUSETTS
885 Providence Hwy, Dedham, MA 02026 — 781-326-5385

MISSOURI
9804 Watson Road, St. Louis, MO 63126 — 314-965-3512

NEW JERSEY
561 U.S. Route 1, Wick Plaza, Edison, NJ 08817 — 732-572-1200

NEW YORK
Relocating. Please call: — 212-754-1110

PENNSYLVANIA
9171-A Roosevelt Blvd, Philadelphia, PA 19114 — 215-676-9494

SOUTH CAROLINA
243 King Street, Charleston, SC 29401 — 843-577-0175

VIRGINIA
1025 King Street, Alexandria, VA 22314 — 703-549-3806

CANADA
3022 Dufferin Street, Toronto, ON M6B 3T5 — 416-781-9131